The Boned Zone

Surviving Urban Predation

A Guide to Living in Dangerous Urban Areas, Including the memoirs and essays:

Ron Bone in the Hood
Ron Bone and the Man
Who is Boning Who?
To Neglect and Disturb
Hos in the Hood

And dozens of other enlightening and uplifting articles on surviving tyranny in its postmodern urban form.

A Forever Autumn Press Book

Books by James LaFond

Nonfiction

The Fighting Edge, 2000
The Logic of Steel, 2001
The First Boxers, 2011
The Gods of Boxing, 2011
All Power Fighting, 2011
When You're Food, 2011
The Lesser Angles of Our Nature, 2012
The Logic of Force, 2012
The Greatest Boxer, 2012
Take Me to Your Breeder, 2014
The Streets Have Eyes, 2014
Panhandler Nation, 2014
The Ghetto Grocer, 2014
American Fist, 2014
Don't Get Boned, 2014
Alienation Nation, 2014
In The Chinks of The Machine, 2014
How the Ghetto Got My Soul, 2014
Saving the World Sucks, 2014

Taboo You, 2014
The Fighting Life, 2014
Narco Night Train, 2014
Into the Mountains of Madness: in [3 volumes], 2014
Incubus of Your Sacred Emasculation, 2014
Breeder's Digest, 2014
The Third Eye, 2015
Modern Agonistics, 2015
By the Wine Dark Sea, 2015
The Pale Usher, 2016
The End of Masculine Time, 2015
War Drums, 2015
A Thousand Years in His Soul: The Poets, 2015
A Thousand Years in His Soul: The Seers, 2015
Of Lions and Men, 2015
Your Trojan Whorse, 2015
On Bitches, 2016
Equidistant Drowning Babies, 2015
Welcome to Harm City, 2015
Waking Up in Indian Country, 2015
The Boned Zone, 2015

A Sickness of the Heart: Part One, 2015
A Sickness of the Heart, Part Two, 2015
Let the Weak Fall, 2015
If I Were King, 2015
Dark Art of an Aryan Mystic, 2015
No B.S. Boxing, 2016
Stick Fighting Fundamentals, 2016
The Sardonyx Stone, 2016
A Dread Grace, 2016
Stillbirth of a Nation, 2016
The Boxer Dread, 2016
The Ghetto Gourmet, 2016
40,000 Years from Home, 2016
The Liver-Eater Reader, 2016

Fiction

Astride the Chariot of Night, 2014
Sacrifix, 2014
Rise, 2014
Motherworld, 2014
Planet Buzzkill, 2014
Fruit of The Deceiver, 2014
Forty Hands of Night, 2014
Black and Pale, 2014
Daughters of Moros, 2014
Darkly, 2014
This Design is Called Paisley, 2015
Hurt Stoker, 2015
Poet, 2015
Triumph, 2015
Winter, 2015
The Spiral Case, 2015
Hemavore, with Dominick Mattero, 2015
Yusuf of the Dusk, 2016
Mantid, 2016
RetroGenesis: Day 1, with Erique Watson, 2015
Easy Chair, 2015
Happily Ever Under, 2015
Road Killing, 2015
Fat Girl Dancing, 2015
Buzz Bunny, 2015
T. Spoone Slickens, Inquire, 2015
Dream Flower, 2015
The Song of Jeannot, 2015
Organa, 2015
A Hoodrat Halloween, 2015
The Consultant, 2015
Reverent Chandler, 2015

He, 2016
Under the Crescent,
2016
Kettle of Bones, 2016

Sunset Saga Novels

Big Water Blood Song,
2011
Ghosts of the Sunset
World, 2011
Beyond the Ember Star,
2012

Comes the Six Winter
Night, 2012
Thunder-Boy, 2012
The World is Our
Widow, 2013
Behind the Sunset Veil,
2013
Den of The Ender, 2013
God's Picture Maker,
2014
Out of Time, 2015
Seven Moons Deep,
2016

For Mary, enjoy the blue skies of Virginia

Contents

The Boned Zone

'The Boned Zone'

Mescaline Franklin's Retrospective on the Harm City Purge and Request for a White Man's Urban Survival Manual

You, know, Baltimore is way ahead of New York and Chicago on murders right now. I like the idea of a few white guys staying in that savage shithole. Maybe becoming a minority is the only thing that's going to save white people from themselves—that we will have to be men again as the lie crumbles around us. When I got back up here everybody thought I was crazy for going to Baltimore with all that going on. The brothers, are like, "You got to be kidding me, Yo, mixing it up with those raw-ass niggers down there."

But I was like, "Hey, I wasn't going to bitch out and not go see my friend because a couple of you savages were fucking up cops. I hate the cops too."

I feel lucky to have been there. For one thing the weather was nice. There was this menace in the air—an empty town where everyone is waiting for the zombies to attack. It was nice—something real instead of the media lies, even if it was scary.

The Boned Zone

And there was those fucking musclehead goons in the black tactical uniforms without the fucked up Baltimore accent, who the hell were those guys? We'll never know. They might have been whacking dudes in Nigeria last month. The experience of facing off with those four huge military guys was pretty cool—like getting to see the tiger at the zoo when you're a kid.

For another there were no cops? I'm always on pins and needles up here that the cops are going to bust me for being the only white guy around. But when we were out down there it was great—no pigs to punish us for fighting back if the savages came. We actually had white people out walking the streets, not afraid—because you know what we are afraid of is getting locked up for defending ourselves. When these savages come for us— like that guy in your old hood that just got stomped— they will be trying to put us away, swinging for the fences. But if we even hurt one of them defending our self we'll have the entire machine come down on us.

What you need to write is a little book about how to defend yourself from these savages without hurting them—like Don't Get Boned, but shorter, and more about surviving The Boned Zone, than avoiding it, which is your normal thing. I'm a BJJ guy, but don't want to be on the ground with one dude getting my head kicked in by another. What are the tactical answers that don't require learning another entire combat art?

I just got a pass—a shield—from a cop, which is a big thing, and might mean the difference between getting arrested or not—I'll explain to you how it works when we get together—but only in this cop's jurisdiction. The savages are so good at gaming the system now, that they're more dangerous as a legal threat than a physical one, so I'm more worried about them than the cops because it's a more comprehensive threat.

You know, everywhere I go—and I get around—where I meet white people and they find out I travel to Baltimore on business, they express the same sentiment, that any indigenous white person who still lives there is either a criminal or a drug addicted low life, that committed that heinous American crime of having roots, and that deserves what they get from the blacks—like being the last white guy in Detroit, means you have to be an asshole like Eminem. White people are so conditioned to buy their way out of a bad area and run that anyone who stands and resist is considered a pariah. Well, with this shit economy more and more or us whites are going to have to stay behind and resist. You've been doing it for decades—and you need to put the answers out there—the tactical masculine answers.

The Boned Zone

All these cities I travel to: Baltimore, Camden, Philly, New York, Detroit and Chicago, they all have the same crime problem: blacks and cops just jacking up whoever they can whenever they can, and generally in restricted areas. The entire numbers game is really just bullshit. Who cares how many crimes for a hundred thousand. If I took the areas where repeat violence occurs in any of these cities, from a half million to fifteen million, and just put them down somewhere as a city—just those black cop-infested neighborhoods—it would look the same.

So, when I'm in one of these cities, where the cops are out hunting black guys and me, and the black guys are out hunting each other and me, what is my best course? Forget about fixing this shit, how do I survive this shit. I liked your coverage of the purge, but it was mostly context. I want to read more about how you deal with that blood thirsty savage, and that power hungry cop, when they are in your face. I spent my life being attacked by blacks when I was a kid—everyday, none-stop, ten to one, for years. Now I have cops fucking with me regularly. It's as if the savages put a taboo mark on me and said 'we're not hunting him anymore,' and the cops see that and they're on me like reserved game at a hunting preserve.

On top of that, with the fact that sixty kids just got a pass for fucking up a bunch of cops and putting twenty of them in the hospital, you know we're next. You, me—every white man who lives in a majority black urban area—is going to be attacked in the near future. I'll buy you beer in perpetuity for writing a manual on surviving that.

I want to know, what do I do when the cops rip the door open and drag me from the car because of the way my hat is cocked, and, most importantly, how to deal with the savages when they come over the wall?

Alright young man, at your request I will begin writing The Boned Zone, one entry at a time, right here, where your mom is not safe, at jameslafond.com. Thanks for providing the preface.

Summer of Hate

The Boned Zone: The Caucasian Guide to Surviving the Black-on-White Urban Race Purge

"James, Gentrification is taking place in the wilds and timbered places in Utah also, except it's the rednecked hillbillies that are being displaced, the rich are buying all the water and land they can lay their greasy hands on, they still need the white trash from the east side of the county to run their infrastructure but we are slowly being replaced by brothers from the south, who will work for less money but take the same abuse. People like my family are retiring and moving to the more abandoned rural areas where they can live on the scraps they throw to us—what the developers have not polluted with the cash they need to ruin our lifestyle. Good luck. I can see the smoke in my dreams at night coming from the cities of the east as they burn to the ground."

-Ishmael, 5/3/15

This book is dedicated to Ishmael, a man with his back to a different kind of wall.

The Boned Zone

Disclaimer

I am not the apex predator I fantasized about as a boy, but the hunted—with a small 'h' at that—an alternately defiant, observant and furtive beast of prey, who has been harried through the streets of Baltimore, Maryland, since 1981. This book is about dealing with my primary foe, the enemy that has threatened and attacked me hundreds of times, to the cops' dozen negative attentions, and my despicable white cousins' three dozen or so attempts to compromise, and even end, this marginal bipedal life.

The book I intend to write will be based on events yet to occur. I am committed to relating these events in an advisory manner, with the aim being preparing those few urban working class whites who yet inhabit the blackened bowels of America's mid-sized cities, to survive the race purge when it gets to their town. I am not conducting a scientific survey, making objective observations, or trying to save anything more than my ass and that of whomever like-minded and like-situated souls might access this as a survival guide.

Don't Get Boned is not about Baltimore, it's about my Baltimore—Harm City; the place that coughed me up and shall one day swallow me. This is a journal of my experiences and observations, as well as those of people like Robert, my coworker who was hospitalized by two black thugs last night. This book will be as fat as life makes it, and shall encompass events from Wednesday evening, May 13, through Friday, the 4th of September, of the wretched year of our Distant Lord, 2015.

I look forward to this project, even as I look forward to what figures to be a hot summer, in more ways than one, the Summer of Hate; someone else's hate, a slice of my fulfilling and interesting fate.

Jeremy Bentham   May 17, 2015 4:22 PM EDT

James, perhaps you should have your IT department set up a crowd fund, so we can contribute to your legal defense should you become the Bernard Goetz or George Zimmerman of Harm City. Sounds like Robert could use some financial help as well.

responds: May 24, 2015 6:59 PM EDT

Nice thought Jeremy.

We are already set for donations. So, when Big Brutha gets me Charles will send the word out and you may click on the picture of him sitting on the milk crate and help a honky out!

Jeremy Bentham   May 15, 2015 2:39 AM EDT

Take care this Summer James. I'm fairly certain though that both Boomy and I will be praying that Dear Jesus up above watch over you.

"You will not fear the terror of night, nor the arrow that flies by day, nor the pestilence that stalks in the darkness, nor the plague that destroys at midday. A thousand may fall at your side, ten thousand at your right hand, but it will not come near you. You will only observe with your eyes and see the punishment of the wicked." -Psalm 91:5-8 (NIV)

"There is a Divine Providence that protects idiots, drunkards, children and the United States of America." – Prince Otto von Bismarck

responds: May 16, 2015 6:20 PM EDT

I just interviewed Robert, and it was worse than I thought. He's got a brain injury. I'll write it up tomorrow. Based on this week I'm wondering if this is a long wind down or a new paradigm.

I have been convinced to begin arming myself, and will do so with an eye on staying out of trouble with the cops—who are still noticeably absent in the county. They have returned to the city in normal force.
Thanks for your prayers Jeremy.

'Who is Boning Who?'

The Harm City Food Chain

I have no numbers to support the following. These are simply the environmental factors that every thinking asshole in this septic city –yes, all four of us—knows to be the driving parameters of Harm City strife.

The list below begins with the most frequent violent relationship and ends with the least frequent. 1-3 are pretty close, to the point that in different parts of town they will be reversed. The list addresses the city and adjacent county as a whole. This is important as the most common type of county violence involves blacks from the city raiding county neighborhoods, while the most common violence in the city is perpetrated by cops, who are often county residents, upon mostly black city dwellers.

No moral judgments are made on the list below, which is simply a frequency of aggression chain of predation.

Clarification

In other writings I have placed black on black violence above cops on blacks. The difference here is I am counting arrests that do no physical harm—which are legion, but impact and drive the predation chain. The reason I am counting legal aggressions that have no intended or effective harm is that this food chain is partially an expression of violence being pushed down. An arrest is violence, is aggression. So, while beatings and shootings of black men by black men vastly outnumber beatings and shootings of black men by cops, in the mind of the black man, every arrest is whitey pushing down on him. And unless he feels like he can take out a cop, then he'll take it out on you white boy.

The Social Sodomy Food Chain

1. The most common form of aggression in Baltimore City/County consist of legal and extra-legal uses of force by mixed race cops against black males, followed closely by

2. Black males on black males, followed closely by,

3. Black males on white males, followed at a great distance by the rest of the idiot on idiot violence parings

4. Mixed race cops on white males

5. Black females on everybody

6. Mixed race cops on black females

7. White females on white males

8. White males on white females

9. Mixed race cops on white females

10. Black males on white females

11. White males on white males

12. Black aggressions against Hispanics—all four genders and legal status' combined

13. Attacks by escaped anacondas on Live Action Role Playing geeks goofing off in city sewers

14. English professors suffering from advanced cataracts molesting fading porn stars at the Sip and Bite diner

15. Attacks by super-soaker armed squeegee kids on U.S. Navy SEALs

16. And, last but not least, a racist white man [that would be Big Chev or Crazy Mark, or WhiteBoy Wayne, if he was not a fictional character] threatening or attacking violent and rude black youths

Know your place on the food chain and you can narrow your threats down to a primary, a secondary, and a tertiary source, and be happier about your predicament as you recover in the emergency room, having correctly guessed who was going to jack you up all along!

MarkB   May 15, 2015 11:35 PM EDT

"...the black women I speak to are...spending time among white men"

again: in my neck of the woods these are the ones getting the beatdown, unless they're high yellows (and even then the yellows are ostracized for 'thinkin they up'). Niggas chase white women, but beat their own if they hookup with a white, asian, or mexican. Nonetheless, I see that you're talking to your target, white men, when it's not listed as a category

responds: May 16, 2015 6:08 PM EDT

To clarify the black girls spending time with white men—who speak to me—are suburban. The ghetto girls say high and smile, and run there mouth at the bar and on the bus. The ghetto girls that I interviewed for The Logic of Steel, The Logic of Force, and When You're Food, I no longer have contact with, as I retired from the ghetto grocer biz, and now work out in the county. The only way for low end black chicks to really speak openly is to gain their trust at work, where they get to see you not being a back stabbing prick for an extended period.

Also, I am in one city, that may be unique in the fact that black women—at least publicly—are doing more violence to black men than the other way around. The exception is black women having black men kill rival black women.

MarkB   May 14, 2015 9:28 PM EDT

no "black males on black females" category? In my neighborhood (60% black) this is a substantial category, even tho many bitches don't snitch about it

JL **responds:** May 15, 2015 10:51 AM EDT

Excellent point.

This is information I don't get much of, and is surely present, as are some other categories I neglected to include. Women do not tell you about attacks by there men until you have done a number of interviews, where a guy will blurt it out. What I and those I interview have witnessed in public is women beating their men and children.

Also this category does not cause violent pushdown against my target readership of predominantly white men.

Currently the black women I speak to are either spending time among white men, or are not experiencing this. Also, with all sub lethal violence among blacks, there is a severe lack of reporting. Two black women that I know of have been killed by black men over the last year in Baltimore, and the media has shown very little interest in their cases.

Paul Rain   May 14, 2015 4:18 PM EDT

Hmm. One suspects the list may get a new addition once the 'spanic population climbs a leedle bit higher.

responds: May 16, 2015 6:24 PM EDT

Ms-13 is in the D.C. area, and have been for a while. I know that is a Salvadoran gang and am not sure of the Mexican Salvadoran ratio in our own Latino population. If a serious Hispanic gang shows up in Baltimore, that will be something to see. We'll be back in the top three for murders then.

Baltimore Race Purge Is Ongoing

And Began A Week Earlier Than Reported

"You gotta love Baltimore—The Wire has got nothing on the real deal. Two years ago I read a stat that said half of the Baltimore PD was on paid leave while awaiting police brutality charges! And who do we have being charged with various crimes resulting in the death of Freddie Gray—but three white cops and three black cops—that's simply precious! What did these guys do? Whose shoes did they step on to deserve this? You know that every cop has done the obligatory planting of a suspect's head into something hard. It's probably a rite of passage with those guys. No way is there a Baltimore City cop who is not guilty of brutality. Freddie Gray is a martyr—they're painting murals about him.

"We get section eight people moving into the neighborhood. They don't work; spend their time casing the place seeing what is worth breaking into or stealing. Crime goes up, then they're gone after a year or two. I see junkies nodding out on the side streets of my neighborhood—and these people are taxing me to pay these cops. Who paid for the [national] Guard? That had to cost. Fuck the cops—and let this city burn—it certainly deserves it. I'll break bad one day, its coming. I've got it in me. You know there's going to be a round two."

-Andrew 'B'more' Metzger

Andrew shares a commonly held opinion in Harm City, that there will be at least one more riot, sooner rather than later. Interestingly it is white suburbanites and urban elves that see no violence on the horizon, only a moral debt owed the helpless children who beat down a city police department.

Me, I could care less about the riots. Rather my interest lies in the purge that ran concurrent with the riots, and now appears to have occurred beginning with the arrest and hospitalization of Freddie Gray a week earlier than I had thought. On April 22nd, on 45th Street in the Dundalk area of Baltimore County, close to the city line, a mob of black teens beat a 61 year old white man nearly to death for trying to stop two girls from fighting on the hood of his car. Five days later the city was burning.

Interestingly commentators felt obliged to point out that the man did not use force—indicating that most Baltimoreans would regard his beating deserved if he actually used force to remove two tussling hoodrats from his vehicle. It is, by the way, common in that neighborhood for cars to be vandalized by these rampaging youths. I spoke with one resident who told me that the cops warned him not to leave anything in his car as it would certainly be broken into. This sentiment is a warning that an effective defense against such an attack could carry legal hazards, of the criminal, federal, and civil kind.

Make no mistake, municipal, state and federal governments all have a reasonable, logical vested interest in you not being permitted to effectively defend yourself. Operate against your enemies with a tactical view, not an emotional view based on notions of fairness, justice, and morality.

The innocent unarmed black teens charged with smashing this man's face in, who broke his eye sockets, and made his brain bleed, are:

Andrew Omar Allen, 15

Yahkeem Zavion Wheatley, 15

Samtoya Isiah Williams, 17

Mya Lashae Stewrat, 17

The Boned Zone

Antoine Willie Lawson, 17

Keenan Tylike Holloway, 20

And some unnamed punk of undetermined age

That is a fairly typical attack pack. Fortunately this attack was filmed, hence it has not been swept under the rug as happens with most black on white pack attacks. Incidentally, in Baltimore, there has not been a white on black attack of this nature since 1996—and those two white boys got away with murder. For the last two decades it has been one way, all the way—black on white, just like newsprint, only it does not make the newspaper in most cases, because poor white men are the least cared about slice of the American pie. So pay attention and apply the threat evaluations and countermeasures used in this series to your own predicament to make sure you do not become the soggy cracker crumbs swept under some left wing politician's rug when it is your turn to be purged

These helpless black youth all came from the city—not a one a county resident. This was a raid, most likely staged at Patterson Park High School, from where black students have raided East Baltimore and Baltimore County, whites with impunity since the mid 1980s. I have since spoken to two more coworkers from East

Baltimore County and one bar patron from my city neighborhood, who were attacked during the run up to the riots.

The purge began earlier, and has lasted longer than the riots—longer by far. Below are my preliminary findings—and please, keep in mind, that I am not researching this, but just passing on what I have witnessed, and what my friends and coworkers have reported. The violence I present here is a tiny sliver of what a reporter would find, if one cared—or was allowed to—inquire.

-Police sirens are still three times more numerous than normal in Northeast Baltimore, with ambulance sirens still sounding twice as often as usual.

-Uptown/out-of-town busses are back up to 80% of normal passengers.

-Cross town buses, running at night, are still only carrying 10-20% of normal passengers.

-Whites and black military age males [BMAMs] are almost completely absent at night.

-City cab and sedan waits for called in rides have gone from 45 minutes to 5 minutes, meaning that cabbies and sedan drivers are circling the area like starving sharks.

The Boned Zone

-One cabbie confided that he has lost 60% of his business since the riots, and that many other cabbies have moved away from Baltimore.

-Visible police presence in Northeast Baltimore has risen to half of normal, and that was never much. Why this is I have no clue.

-In the Essex precinct of the county, I normally see one cop cruiser every half mile at night, and one per a mile during the day. Day time coverage has returned to normal, but nighttime police presence in Essex is still at about zero to 30% of normal, depending on the night.

-The demeanor of nearly every person out and about at night, black or white, city or county, is anxious, visibly anxious.

I did not expect this. The police absence is not a bother to me, and could have to do with officers taking flex time, as overtime was not being paid to city cops during the purge. However, the purge of lone whites by groups of blacks is ongoing, and will be detailed in future entries. When Robert gets out of the hospital I will interview him about the incident that put him out of work last night, May 13, when two innocent unarmed black teens attacked him as he sat on the front porch of his county home just blocks away from where the 61 year old man was purged on April 22.

'Stepping Off The Hate Train'

Just For A Minute, Before Getting All Righteous Again

Last night I was taking my break behind Bubba's register when Al, the bread vender, stopped by and began ranting and raving about the recent attacks on whites, about all of the taxes he pays going to breed violent welfare punks that will someday rob him. He totally cannot figure me out, living in the dark city, grossing less than half of what he pays in taxes.

Al makes a lot of sense until you find out he has a double standard. He began cheering the fact that three white guys from a Pennsylvania town near his home recently beat a Mexican to death. Al considers himself a moderate 'Libertarian-leaning conservative,' yet he believes in mob rule via violent purging, so long as it is white guys doing the purging.

The collective wisdom in our society is that only white guys like Al can be hateful to the point of acting on their racist beliefs, and that black youths are merely misguided mirrors of the white man's perennial hate.

However, this time last week I spoke to a black man who is an elementary school principal, who suggested that bricking white ladies in the head and demolishing some guy's retail store is justified so long as some white guy told a black protester to get a job.

Bubba looked at me when Al left, and shook his head, demonstrating that he had not been swayed by Al's argument that all black people are violent fiends.

I have explained to Bubba that these older racist guys are society's poison, the world's half-assed nod to tribalism that stops right at 'us versus them' and never adopts any of the primal tribal values that are so much bigger, deeper, and more useful than Al's pedestrian hate. The true sin of such hatred, in my eyes, is that it often leads to clouded tactical judgment and inaccurate strategic assessments.

When you see the world as Al does, as good shining white and bad midnight black, you deprive yourself of an appreciation of the nuanced nature of the threat you face, which limits your action menu to the clumsiest methods. Al is hiding in a small rural town, which is how most white racists deal with their hate, by running away from the object of that crippling emotion. This sissy end of a man's fighting heart, is the reason why primitive warrior societies cultivated cults of honor, based on respect for an enemy.

The warrior who merely hates his enemy becomes as if a woman, whose job it was to hate in primitive societies. When captives were brought home for torture they were typically given to the women as they were renowned for their cruelties. Women are cruel to rivals for the very same reason sissies revel in hatred of an enemy, because they get carried away on the wings of emotion and forget that a man is foremost a tactical creature, and that emotions like hate make of him a woman, hiding in his fairytale cottage, like Al, on the Pennsylvania state line.

And finally, hatred thwarts a man's ability to make useful alliances with those best positioned to help him achieve his goals, those who have one foot in his world and one foot in the enemy's world.

Jeremy Bentham   May 19, 2015 7:34 PM EDT

The Leftists are very skillful at using rhetoric to confuse issues and to silence their opposition. They tell you not to "hate", when they themselves are filled with hatred for anything and everything normal, traditional and/or successful. The Lefties will kick you in the balls and poke you in the eye and then tell you with a straight face how very bad it is to kick people in the balls and poke them in the eye. Our President is especially accomplished at this type of Leftist rhetorical duplicity and intellectual dishonesty: http://www.nationalreview.com/article/398283/snark er-chief-victor-davis-hanson. Who would have imagined that race relations in America would actually become worse, AFTER the majority of white Americans elected a black man as their President? Twice even! Now we are all to believe that the reason for all the crime and poverty in the black community is because white people suck? Don't buy that if you want to live white folks!

Jeremy Bentham   May 19, 2015 7:31 PM EDT

Yes James, the Holy Bible is full of good military quotes, as well as good military advice. Everything from strategies for deploying armies down to individual common task skills. For example, the effective use of challenge and pass word (071-331-0801, U.S. Army Warrior Task Skill Level I) is described in Judges 12:4-6. The Judges were actually warlords, military commanders appointed to lead the tribes of Israel. As military commanders they had judicial power to reward and punish everyone, warrior and non-combatant, placed under their authority, hence the title "judge" as translated from the Hebrew. The Twelve Tribes of Israel were a people under arms (every able-bodied man was a warrior) surrounded by enemies back then (not dissimilar to the modern nation of Israel). Contrary to popular belief today, Judaism and Christianity are NOT pacifist religions. Modern pacifism entails the doctrine that one should not employ force or violence even in self-defense. Judaism and Christianity are merely "non-violent", eschewing aggressive violence as a just and acceptable means of getting what you want from others.

When Jesus suggested to his disciples that they "turn the other cheek" he was stating that they did not need to accept a challenge to fight (symbolized by the slap on the cheek); just as Stoic philosophers, like Epictetus, suggested that any insult, injury or embarrassment one might suffer from such an act resided mainly in one's own mind. Does the "turn the other cheek" admonition then mean that you must suffer major evil without resisting, like letting someone chop off your hand or the hands of your wife and children? I think we all know the answer to that. Judaism and Christianity follow the doctrine of "universal benevolence" (AKA the Golden Rule), that is to treat other humans, even those not a member of our own tribe, in the kind and benevolent manner most of us wish to be treated ourselves. The "Golden Rule" even predates the life and ministry of Jesus and was promoted by many others, including Buddha, Confucius, Plato and the Stoics. Much erroneous pacifist dogma (Judaic, Christian and secular humanist) comes from the fact that the original meaning of the Sixth Commandment has been often mistranslated. In the original Hebrew the Sixth Commandant states "Lo Tirtzach": meaning "No murder" or do not murder. For some reason the 40 some scholars that King James commissioned to compile the English language translation of the Holy Bible that bears his name (i.e. The King James Version or KJV) translated the Sixth Commandment as "Thou shalt not kill". There is big difference between the two translations, the former making a clear distinction between justified and unjustified homicide. This misinterpretation alone caused no end of confusion and disagreement over the centuries. The New International Version (NIV) of the Holy Bible, a modern English translation, on the other hand correctly translates the

Sixth Commandment as "You shall not murder". Rabbi Dovid Bendory of JPFO provides a good discussion on the correct interpretation of the Commandment and how false pacifist dogmas should not prevent one from engaging in righteous and effective self-defense: http://jpfo.org/rabbi/6th-commandment.htmhttp://jpfo.org/rabbi/6th-commandment.htm. Just as the Commandment tells us not to murder others, we should also not engage in "self-murder", AKA "suicide". In particular we should not adopt suicidal social and political doctrines or imagine that Judeo-Christian religion or the U.S Constitution are suicide pacts for our own people and our own Western culture: http://pjmedia.com/victordavishanson/multicultural-suicide/.

Jeremy Bentham   May 19, 2015 6:57 PM EDT

[Quirt and Randy are getting ready to leave the First day meeting. Randy is reading aloud from the Bible given to Quirt by the Quakers]

Randy McCall: Listen to this: "And Benaiah, the son of Jehoiada, the son of a valiant man of Kabzeel, who had done many acts of valor, slew two men of Moab and went down and slew three lions in the midst of a pit in the time of snow."

Randy McCall: [to Quirt] Whew, three lions!

Randy McCall: [continues reading] "And Benaiah slew an Egyptian who had a sword. He took away his sword and slew him with a staff... " I guess that must mean a club. Oh, brother, this is good writing!

Quirt Evans: Let's go!

Randy McCall: What about the Bible? You can't throw it away, that would be bad luck.

Quirt Evans: Then keep it!

Randy McCall: Alright. This is one book I'm sure gonna read.

"Angel and the Badman", starring John Wane as Quirt Evans, 1947. FYI: the Bible verse cited is from 2 Samuel 23.

responds: May 24, 2015 6:52 PM EDT

And that is my favorite bible passage— Benaiah the badass.

Thanks

Jeremy Bentham   May 15, 2015 2:05 AM EDT

"One acts decisively only in the conviction that all the angels are on one side and all the devils on the other." - Saul Alinsky Rules for Radicals 1971, Tactics — P.134

"Hatred is an element of struggle; relentless hatred of the enemy, that impels us over and beyond the natural limitations of man and transforms us into effective, violent, selective and cold killing machines. Our soldiers must be thus: a people without hatred cannot vanquish a brutal enemy."

-Ernesto "Che" Guevara

"Generals think war should be waged like the tourneys of the Middle Ages. I have no use for knights; I need revolutionaries."
-Adolf Hitler

"Winston Churchill's remarks to his private secretary a few hours before the Nazis invaded the Soviet Union graphically pointed out the politics of means and ends in war. Informed of the imminent turn of events, the secretary inquired how Churchill, the leading British anti-communist, could reconcile himself to being on the same side as the Soviets. Would Churchill find it embarrassing and difficult to ask his government to support the communists? Churchill's reply was clear and unequivocal: "Not at all. I have only one purpose, the destruction of Hitler, and my life is much simplified thereby. If Hitler invaded Hell I would at least make a favorable reference to the Devil in the House of Commons."
- Saul Alinsky Rules for Radicals 1971, Tactics — P.29.

"I pursued my enemies and crushed them; I did not turn back till they were destroyed. I crushed them completely, and they could not rise; they fell beneath my feet. You armed me with strength for battle; you humbled my adversaries before me. You made my enemies turn their backs in flight, and I destroyed my foes. They cried for help, but there was no one to save them—to the Lord, but he did not answer. I beat them as fine as the dust of the earth; I pounded and trampled them like mud in the streets." -2 Samuel 22:38-43 (NIV)

responds: May 16, 2015 6:22 PM EDT

As usual, the bible says it best. Nothing like Old Testament war quotes.

'Let Randy Die on the Side of the Road'

Dealing With Violent White Trash in a Black Ruled Crime Zone

Tony, Jimmy and Robert are clerks I work with at night, sometimes helping them sort their freight. Jimmy and Tony drive scooters to work and chain them at the end of the sidewalk against the cart guard. Robert is Tony's older brother, the most physical guy of the bunch—a good guy that doesn't mind breaking a sweat. Last night, when Tony told me that Robert, age 46, had been beaten up on his porch by two young black guys, and was in the hospital, I asked him if he had had any trouble lately.

You will notice a common thread to these two stories. The basic reason for these attacks amounts to paying it downward, down the food chain. The two perps are white drug addicts who are beholding to the blacks from the city that control the Essex drug trade. They get there asses robbed, and beaten so often that they can't wait for a chance to jack up someone—and that someone is not going to be a cop or a black dude. For one thing, the only black guys that travel alone are insane, or armed. Tony and Jimmy are small and not athletic, easy marks, it would seem, for a crack head in need of a self esteem boast and a scooter.

"Yeah, but just from white guys, if you can believe that. Like they don't have anything better to do. Druggies, both of them. The one guy came up on me while I was securing my scooter, pointed at the key, and said, 'I'll take that.'

"I said, 'No you won't pal.'

"He stepped forward, so I stepped back and drew my case cutter, and he backed off, telling me I had to worry and what he was going to do to me if he caught me away from the store. [When I was a store manager I was like a heat seeking missile on these low life scum that harassed my help—who had it bad enough working for an asshole like me—and chased a few down the street.]

"Now the thing with Jimmy happened when we still had police around here. He locks his scooter up—just had a new pack put on it. This crackhead comes up on the walk and tells him it's in the way. Jimmy said, 'No it's not. Step around.'

"Then, 'Bam!' that crackhead kicked his scooter over and cracked the pack. Jimmy was like, 'What the heck!' and the guy went off on him, screaming like bloody murder, carrying on like a black person. I was calling the cops while Jimmy was squaring up with him.

"Before it came to blows those two big badass cops who came and got that stupid shoplifter, they roll up, walk up to the dude, and say to us while they're staring at him, "Well guys, meet Randy. Randy is a piece of shit. Randy is a menace to the people of Hawthorne and Essex. If you ever see Randy you can beat his ass and we'll look the other way. It's open season on his punk ass. If you ever see Randy bleeding to death on the side of the road, let Randy die on the side of the road!'

"Randy left!"

Ruling Inferior Whites on the Street

For the most part—unless you're dealing with a big insane dude like Crazy Mark, you can beat the dog shit out of any white trash dude that gives you shit. Make sure you break his thumb and forefinger after you drop him in case he has access to a gun. These kind of guys don't go to the hospital. They either go get high [the most common course of action] or go get something that's going to help them get even. You generally don't have to worry about them bringing friends like the black guys, but a weapon, so stomp on their hands until the back of the hand feels like broken pretzels under your boot heel.

The cops won't give a shit—they're white.

Trashy white dudes are also a way to build your rep. If you are walking in a drug market to, let's say get your cheese pizza, and one of these fiends tries to shake you down so he can buy another hit from the black guys that run the corner, paint the curb with his face and get rancid on him—not loudly, but quietly. You should not say anything loud enough for anybody but him to hear.

Do not go too heavy on the head area, but break ankles and hands, if you're a BJJ guy have fun separating something. Crippling white trash dudes is good for building the menace required to survive the blacks. For one thing, even the lowest black dudes have family that will avenge them. Not so the poor whites, they're alone generally.

Make them more alone.

Make them die inside.

Break them.

They are backstabbing traitors who have tried to prey on one of their own as an alternative to standing up to their enemy.

The only mercy they deserve is whatever is required to keep your ass out of jail.

Above all, brutalizing your white inferiors when they get out of line will help you blow off some of that steam you are always bottling up when facing down gangs of blacks and dealing with the cops giving you shit for being a man and walking like a human being.

One thing that should not be overlooked is the intelligence value of white dopers. If you need to hit a black dude that has aggressed against a loved one, then these guys have the info on where and when to catch him alone. So long as the inferior white does not touch or threaten you it is preferable to break him with your mind, and leave his body intact. It is not difficult to develop a limited type of loyalty in one of these worm-ridden hearts with a few acts of kindness, once you have put them in their place.

outside   May 17, 2015 3:27 PM EDT

When things get this bad I would prefer a more genocidal solution.

responds: May 24, 2015 7:08 PM EDT

Most human leaders throughout history
would agree with you.
We seem to be in an anomalous social
state.

'This Wretchedness Up In Here'

One Man's Monologue on Urban Blight and Mass Transit

I thought mass transit would be back to normal last night. On Friday night the bus wasn't even leaving the city, but dead ending in the ghetto, so I returned home, and called the boss, telling him I'd be in for the morning shift instead. I figured that would be the last MTA hiccup left over from the riots—and I suppose it was. The real problem is almost no one is riding the bus at night any more.

Of the 25 blacks and 5 Mexicans normally on the bus there were 4 blacks and 1 Mexican, just like during the riots! These are working people. The cab drivers are starving—not that people in our bracket can afford $50 cab fares for working a $60 shift.

Where are they?

The odd thing was how they all stared at me—except for the Mexican Mama, whose daughter is usually with her; a real pretty young thing who is forever getting asked out on dates by the black guys. For an answer she has two things programmed on her smart phone, in large print English. The first one is, 'I Don't Speak English.' If they persist she pulls up, 'I AM MARRIED!' If they keep it up after that Mama gives them the eye, and they back off. Mama's probably the baddest person on the bus. I could well imagine her taking us all out with a fish knife. Mama does not stare at me, just gives me that, 'You have given me no reason to summon my sons, so you may pass Gringo,' look of alien matriarchal ire.

The blacks, however, all regulars except for one well dressed gay dude, bugged their eyes out as if I was a four-armed white Barsomian ape.

None of the 1-3 hoodlums that occasionally afflict us were there.

Where was everyone?

I decided to go to sleep, with my back to the plexi-shield before the rear door. When I opened one eye the black girl across from me, who usually travels with a mangina, was just staring at me in amazement. I nodded off for a while, then the gay dude started running his prissy mouth to a girl, who happened to be one of his employees at an upscale clothiers in Towson, headed home to Essex—which he should have just about worked his way out of. Since I could not go to sleep I took notes:

"Look at this wretchedness up in here. This is the most ghetto place you ever didn't wanna be! They need to infuse some money into this mess. I normally bypass all of this blight on the highway, but I lost my car in all that stupidity [the riots] week before last. I'll be getting a ride through CarMax in a few days, so I'll be with you for the rest of the week. Where is everybody? This can't be it—ain't no holiday."

Young lady: "Nobody has been on the busses at night since that mess. It's creepy out. I got my boyfriend picking me up at the stop."

Manager: "Sweet Jesus, would you look at the colors on that's strip mall? They need to fix that. You know strip malls are coming back. Malls like we work at are a thing of the past—good God look at that bank up to the Wal-Mart, take a million Mexicans to clean that shit up. This is a blight. How can people live like this?"

As Mexican Mama gets off, the girl answers, "Oh it's terrible out here. You go to the shoe store over there, and those trifling people won't even say hello when you walk through the door. People over here are all about the EBT [food stamps] WIC and so on."

Manger: "That is pathetic. We sold a five hundred dollar pair of shoes tonight. You better believe you don't do that without a smile and a polite greeting. What is this world coming to?"

I ran out of receipt paper and nodded off. When I woke up and offloaded only three patrons remained and the major transfer point was empty, except for one man hanging out behind the shelter I was passing. The three cops I usually see in route to work were nowhere to be seen. As I hit the 7-11 it occurred to me that I need to start carrying my hickory cane, or make some other provision. It feels like another world, a world I may very well prefer over the one that died three weeks ago, a world that is not going to let me off easy for being unarmed.

'Sir, It Is Rough Out There!'

Boomy on The Nigerian Cabbie Exodus from Baltimore, Corrupt City Government, and 'Mister and Mrs. Yuppie'

Having arrived to work bemused by the lack of traffic, cops, and bus passengers, I was wondering what this meant. I had gotten a drive to work from Daniel on Monday so had not been in position to observe this slice of my world a full two weeks after the purge and riots supposedly ended. I would find out on Thursday morning that virtually no school students—college, county, or city—were using the bus, or had, since the affair ended. Only in the later days of the riots were they using the buses. Now I seem to be viewing a different way of life, an absence of mass transit use after dark and by students.

About 1 a.m., two hours early, Boomy, the Nigerian cab driver, who saved 'the blonde woman of the yuppies' from two different gangs of rampaging black men 16 days ago, came by the dairy case and said, "Good evening, Sir."

I then asked him a few questions and he was off and running in his engaging style.

"Sir, I have lost sixty percent of my business since the riots—those fool people attacking the police as if that will make a good end. The interesting thing is that my associates and relatives, they all saw it coming. I knew that these men had left over the course of March and April, saying that they were at high risk among your violent niggers. We of Nigeria, Sir, come here as men of God under Jesus to make our bread and serve your people in doing so. We come legal. We come with money. We invest. We work."

"If I may, Sir [looks up with open hand], hand to God, I mean no disrespect, and am blessed to come to your homeland. But your niggers, Sir, they are spoiled and need to be gathered up and shipped back to Africa, where they should be exchanged for good black men and women. The government spoils your niggers, so that all they know is to take. This was the predicament of my associates, eight men in all, of good Nigerian stock.

"They are the younger men, I the elder. They service the general population and tourists. I service the yuppies and the tourists. The one young fellow—a good family man of hard toil, like a son to me—he told me, 'Boomy, I must leave. The blacks are threatening us. You know what this means. They take the good blacks down and run us off, and then they go after the whites—just as it always is in Africa. Then, after the whites with money are scared away, there is no work left.'

"And so it is now. He called me from Houston, and other of our associates called me from the towns they have moved to. They wanted to know if I was still here, still alive in Baltimore. Thank God I do not live in Baltimore, but out here in the suburbs. Is this not why you live here, Sir, out of the city?"

[I inform him of my low rent urban location.]

"Oh, Sir, with kindness and respect, I say to you that the city is not worthy of your residence. But I see you are straight-backed. Be careful. Look at the video I took, Sir. [Shows smart phone video of 21 boarded up shops in the Fell's Point neighborhood.] Take precautions in your travels, Sir, so that we do not lose you."

[I speak to him about the glamour photo of the mayor at Jimmy's Diner in Fells Point.]

"Sir, with respect, your mayor is not a good woman. She is a racist whore. I go to City Hall every month to pay my taxes. The mayor instituted a tax of twenty five cents for every fare. I fill out my paperwork and take it to City Hall. I wait behind one lady, and then get to the counter. The lady is this wide, Sir, six hundred pounds! Polite and well-dressed, Sir, but six hundred pounds. The office is full of big black women dressed in finery. She taps away at her keyboard with her oriental fingernails, and says, 'May I help you?'

"I comply, present my log, she gives me my tax bill, and I take it to the cashier. In the meantime this man in a suit comes in, dressed like James Bond, Sir, a black man in a well-heeled suit. He carries a large case. As I approach the cashier this man is selling her cakes—a half a cake for three dollars—strawberry, lemon, chocolate, and all of the women, including the supervisor, are all coming over to buy their cake. Now this man, dressed like that, selling cakes, makes one wonder if strawberry is marijuana, lemon cocaine, and chocolate heroin! It was a thing of astonishment to see.

"Finally, I make my payment, and return to have my receipt stamped, and there she is, six-hundred pounds, making love to her strawberry cake, and making me wait for another hour while she loves over it and buys more, from this unlikely man in a suit. That, Sir, is your city government. Eating cake like Marie Antoinette as the ashes of your city's hope smolder!

The Boned Zone

"The city has been set back with a terrible blow, and I may not be able to continue on here. The man at the hotel downtown who I contract with, he has lost four— four, Sir—conventions. The tourists are not coming. Thankfully I also service the yuppies of Fell's Point and Canton: Mister Yuppie going to and from his cigar shop and whiskey bar, Mrs. Yuppie going to her salon and bistro.

"All else that is left is the homeboys, with their hands in their pockets asking for a ride as if they are prepared for robbery. If I refuse to pick them up they will toss the stone like they did to my associates. So I say, 'Look friend, I am on a call, but I am calling you a cab right now, see?' and I make the call as I pull off, giving him the wink of friendship, knowing that he would rob at gunpoint or stone me at the first opportunity. Then, when out of range, I tell the dispatcher not to make the pickup, that it is too dangerous."

"It is a dangerous town, more so than before the riots. Sir, it is rough out there! My associates saw the writing on the wall and made an exodus. I remain hanging on— thanks to Jesus above—through my yuppie customers. But if the tourists do not return, perhaps I must leave."

In order to stay out of the ever mobile Boned Zone, wherever you reside, speaking to mass transit and cab operators is an excellent source of intelligence. Cabs are as often used by wounded crime victims—those still ambulatory—as are ambulances. For one thing they are quicker and cheaper. Gathering intelligence is the first step toward forming an action plan. Begin with those who work in close proximity to crime, and preferably in the business of operating the type of transportation used by the light guerilla infantry that constitute the purge strike teams in America's urban centers. Other good sources of info are security guards and managers at local retail outlets which see a lot of traffic, such as liquor stores, drug stores, convenience stores and supermarkets.

Adam Swinder   May 15, 2015 6:22 PM EDT

I really want to meet Boomy now, he sounds like an excellent person. A pitcher of beer will be his should we ever meet.

responds: May 16, 2015 6:11 PM EDT

I'll ask him if he drinks. I bet he does not, Sir.

Living Under Tyrone Crow?

Why Beating Whitey Is Legal and Moral: Exposing the Misunderstood Psyche of an Atheistic Society in Decline

Americans—even Atheists—believe that we live in a nominally Christian society. As much as Atheists beat up on Christianity, one would think these two ideologies were polar opposites. However, seen from a primal viewpoint, atheism is a divergent strand of Christianity, competing over the same minds, on the same ethical grounds. How often do we hear atheists attacking Aristotle, The Buddha, Black Elk, Deginawida, Marcus Aurelius, Celtic spiritualists?

In my cracked mind, that is because Modern Christians and Atheists hold the same two values preeminent, and compete over those masses of humanity conditioned to hold these values sacred: the preservation and extension of human life, and the quality of physical existence on earth based on material terms, whereby starvation, pain, homelessness, unemployment and lack of education are absent or minimized.

Contrast this to spiritualists who deny the value of such a cozy, sheltered, well fed and long lingering life, and extol the value of suffering, abstinence, discipline and the transformative experience—which is doctrinally denied to most Christians until after death, and is universally denied to all atheists, who primarily differ with Christians in the matter of the afterlife and the question of an intelligent creator entity.

I suspect that the deep lack of understanding of the urban American ethical matrix is due to Christians not realizing that they are atheists, and hence standing bemused, and that atheists do not realize the depth of their Christian roots, and are thus absolutely ignorant of the fact that they are engineering the deification of their meddling collective will through their untiring efforts to supersize The State as a universal ethos enabler.

Of course you disagree with me. So let me abandon this course of discussion and examine those human behaviors in which I see Christian-Atheism expressed in daily urban life. Once you have considered these collective Christian-Atheistic values as expressed through violent behavior, perhaps you will consider my possession [I was supposed to type 'position,' but have become quite a fan of the Freudian typo, and am keeping it] anew, or perhaps modify your own. The idea behind this exercise is an establishment of an understanding as to how and why one ends up in The Boned Zone.

The broad answer to why you are being brutalized in a street attack, is that you are being collectively boned by the entire corrupt social structure, the nature of which your supposedly less enlightened attackers are far more aware of then you—who believe in concepts that do not exist, such as fairness, rights, and the peculiar American myth that the State somehow serves the cause of individual liberty, when it is itself constructed exclusively at the expense of individual liberty.

The Four True American Values

The values expressed below are those held by collective postmodern American society. These are not urban American values, or black values, but values held in common by all branches of government, the media, the clergy, and most professional thinkers, including men as diverse as Libertarians and leftist liberals. These values are included in this urban survival handbook because the only segment of the American population that has achieved a proper understanding of our collective across the board Christian-Atheistic value system are urban blacks, who, if they find you vulnerable in their ethical zone, will apply these values to you, often by way of a subsidized shoe.

The following values are descendent, with the lower numbered 'greater' values absolutely trumping higher numbered 'lesser' values to the point of utter invalidation.

1. Human life is the most sacred aspect of life on earth, and everything else is subservient to it. Killing a human is a universal sin that may only be forgiven if the killing was committed by a representative of the collective.

2. Quality of human life is second only to life itself. This includes the right to access any and all material goods and benefits desired by the living.

3. The will of the collective is the 3rd pillar of this ethos. The primary aim of the collective will is to make certain that the free will of individuals, including transcendent experiences [drug use and risk taking] and the selfish desire to be free of coercion, do not, in any way, impinge upon the quality of life, or length of life, of the individual or others. The collective protects you first from yourself, and secondly protects others from your false notion of autonomy.

4. Free will, liberty and their expressions, such as freedom to travel free of restraint, freedom to self medicate, property rights, etc., are all trumped by the collective will.

The way this system works in practice is like so:

A person who believes in their right to own a smart phone and to walk freely through Baltimore is mistaken, as the majority of Baltimoreans will deny that right by either attacking him, or by blaming him for the attacker's actions—as the attacker is a member of the collective and has no agency—and denying the individual practicing free will any right to defend himself with force exceeding that force used by the attacker, meaning that he may not walk through Baltimore without committing a crime against his attacker, as equal force cannot establish his free will, but rather bind him in a nasty situation.

For instance, when a Subaru Outback was stopped by a gang of thugs in the Baltimore Inner Harbor last month, and the driver attempted to use the superior force provided by the automobile, he was promptly attacked by the local black collective, and condemned by the political/media white collective for threatening the quality of life of the thugs, for quality of life is known to be reduced when struck by an automobile. If you drive anywhere in the U.S. and are stopped by a gang, and essentially held hostage in your car, any action on your part that injures one of the aggressors will exceed the crime against your fee will, which is secondary to every other American's physical quality of life.

Recently, when recounting the brutal beating of a coworker by four black thugs, I was told by a white liberal that it was not their fault, but his fault, for improperly communicating his desire to help them. The trade off for the protection of the collective is a loss of agency. According to the collective those who do not live according to the fantasy of rights, although privileged with protection against those who would deny access to goods falsely identified as property under that free will delusion, are regarded by the collective will as mere ciphers without agency. The genius of this ethos is that the collective, while simultaneously blaming a polite white tourist for his own attack and defending his black thug attacker, denies the agency [which, to a primal person would be his very soul] of both parties.

For instance, when a black man recently punched a white woman and took her smart phone, it was not his fault, but hers. Her bloody nose was offset by his enrichment, constituting the type of essentially legal transaction that occurs in the ghetto, where beatings are not regarded as immoral, or punished by the law as a crime, unless they result in maiming or death. If she were to try and retain the smart phone—falsely and unjustly defined as property, which is a sick fantasy—with a firearm she would face an indictment and or civil suit and possible federal charges.

Put bluntly, in pre civilized societies, free will is the top value, and anyone who would seek to punch, steal from, or imprison a warrior or his woman, of any race or tribe, could expect to be slain. In our denatured livestock society, where every person is a beast of the State, free will is the least important value, with the physical shell of what might have been a human in ages past, providing the only ethical basis for laws enforced by the collective will.

The root reason why so many whites find themselves in The Boned Zone when attempting to negotiate urban environments, is the fact that the urban underclass—having been subjected to the criminal code for generations—have a clear reality based understanding of the rules of behavior, and these rules of behavior are descendent, being the code of the slave, the peasant, the serf and servant, rising up into the collective consciousness as society declines. Therefore, in Baltimore, a beating—even a severe one—is not regarded as a crime by blacks or law enforcement, unless it produces a cripple or a body. For this reason beatings are casually dispensed, and any escalation of force response is taboo.

Being held against you will be a strong man is not sufficient cause to punch him.

Being punched by a strong man is not sufficient cause to stab him.

Being threatened with death by a man kicking in your front door is not sufficient cause to shoot him, unless he is armed with a weapon.

Aristocratic values, based as they were on warrior codes, recognized an ascending ethos of retaliation: with an insult eliciting a slap, a slap eliciting a duel, etc. the purpose and effect of such systems insured infrequent mob violence within a society, and the rarity of casual force, such as barring a man's way, robbing him empty handed knowing that it is unlawful for him to be armed, or to escalate force, etc.

As Western States built their war machines it was noted that the officer class—descended from the former warrior class and reserving honor codes that recognized ascendant force—were killing each other in duels, inhibiting the growth of the necessarily massive war machines required of mercantile [material based] empires. Nothing is more an affront to the power of the State, than to recognize the 'rights' of its human livestock to duel to the death over points of honor and free will—the later being a reprehensible notion in any case.

Imagine a beef farmer permitting his bulls to fight each other?

To establish the most massive herd a cattlemen segregates the choicest bulls as studs and castrates the rest of the bulls, making them easily led steers.

Black Urban Violence Trends in Baltimore

The State is run on identical principals to a beef herd. Oddly though, most Caucasian subjects of the American State continue to believe in the fantasy of rights handed down by their so-called Founding Fathers. When these people come into contact with those African Americans whose ancestors were owned and brutalized by these same Founding Fathers, they come face to face with individuals born to a people with an historically ingrained appreciation for the nature of State Force, and the adaptability common to surviving minority under classes in any society.

The Boned Zone

The black man knows that beating up a white man is not a crime, while the white man thinks it is, as he retains his free will fantasy. For this reason blacks have almost entirely dispensed with the use of firearms except as arms in drug turf wars.

Since I wrote my first series of violence books, the mandatory firearm penalty in Maryland has resulted in the following trends in black violence:

1. Gun armed robberies of whites are down

2. Shootings of rival blacks are stable

3. Beatings of whites are up

4. Beatings of blacks are stable

5. Stabbings by whites are down

6. Stabbing by blacks—mostly on blacks—are up

7. Mass attacks/stompings by whites are down

8. Mass attacks/stompings by blacks are up

These trends are a response to two factors:

1. Mandatory additional time served for any crime committed with a handgun

2. Increased social tolerance—by blacks and whites—of beatings and public mass attacks by blacks, on anyone. It is just as acceptable for a black mob to beat a black man as to beat a white one. By my count, 1 in 4 black boys are beaten by a group of their fellows before age 16, and most black men are attacked by two or more black men as adults. None of this gets into law enforcement databases due to the antipathy between blacks and law enforcement.

The black Baltimore man or youth of 2015 is more likely to beat and stomp a white person, and less likely to suffer legally from it, than the black man or youth of 1995, who was primarily interested in using a firearm to threaten whites out of their money and automobile, and to kill rival black criminals.

Living Under Tyrone Crow?

Understand, that where it was once socially and legally acceptable for a white man or men to beat a black man, it is now so for the black, who, as long as he stops short of killing the white man, will face no significant legal or social or penalty. Additionally, the violent black actor has significant free legal resources available, just as the white man once had in the form of an all male white jury. It has taken from 1943 to 2015 for leftist agitators, media and judiciary, working as a hammer and anvil social force with reactionary rightist law enforcement agencies, to finally create a black American social consciousness as dedicated to the rule of fear, as was the white American social consciousness that preceded it. Balance in civilized society rarely lasts long, with the State resting most comfortably on a foundation of gross inequity.

Any white man in need of defending himself in a black urban environment must realize that he is defending against a protected class of person, and must be as circumspect about his actions as the working class man of old defending himself against the haughty aristocrat, lest he bring the machinery of the collective will down on his head. The advice in Don't Get Boned is weighted toward the legally defensible course, for no other reason than the fact that the author is not a materialist but a spiritualist; and is therefore less concerned with the pain sustained by the fleshy organism he is trapped in, than having that same bucket of bones used to imprison him in some government mind sodomizing institution. Don't get locked up for defending yourself against an innocent victim of white oppression.

Don't be that guy.

White men do not yet have it as bad as the black man of 100 years ago. It is not yet okay to kill white people. We have yet to have the death of a white man made into a public spectacle with rappers posing with the corpse of some poor white sap. I will make a prediction though, based on the way the racial winds are blowing. Before 2030, a white man will be publicly beaten to death by a black mob, with the video posted online, and the Department of Justice will not pursue hate crime indictments against the proud killers.

Don't be that guy.

We have a new violence paradigm in Baltimore, based on manipulating the ethical delusions of whites and the cumbersome legal system, in order to expand the individual black urban male's opportunities to use force against soft individual targets while avoiding harsh collective penalties. If one were a cynic, one might cite this as a corrective social design for curtailing individual liberty. But here in Harm City, the sky is always blue, the birds are always singing, and the steamy soot-soaked wind is ever at my back!

Billy　November 16, 2015 1:16 PM EST

Come hasn't this video happened already repeatedly?

Blacks kill whites *daily* and I have yet to read or hear about and blacks being prosecuted for the obvious hate crimes they commit on such a regular basis.

I have nowhere near the sympathy you have for the black savages... (and I realize that you don't have much).

Blacks continually prove that they really aren't the same animal as most of the other races. They should be kept away from those of us that are civilized. They are not.

Jeremy Bentham   May 19, 2015 10:39 PM EDT

I recommend that all the working class white people living in Baltimore move to Detroit. Colonize Detroit! On the down side Detroit is, like Baltimore, a crime ridden hell-hole with a majority black population (about 73%) and the city is completely broke having been mismanaged by Liberal Democrats for over fifty years. It also has much colder winters than Baltimore. On the plus side you can buy a house there for a hundred bucks. You can amuse yourself by golfing your way across the uninhabited regions of the city (of which there are many): http://www.bing.com/videos/search?q=golfing+across+detroit&FORM=VIRE2#view=detail&mid=A3EA922F5E6E0AA54CCEA3EA922F5E6E0AA54CCE.And last, but must importantly, the gun laws of the state of Michigan are much more "liberal", as in guaranteeing ordinary citizens the liberty to own and use guns in self-defense. This makes for a much more level playing field than currently exists in Baltimore. The concealed carry permit in Michigan is "shall issue", meaning if you have a clean record and you take the required safety classes you cannot be denied one. Consequently the employed citizens of Detroit have racked up quite a body count recently against home invaders and carjackers: http://www.newsmax.com/US/detroit-guns-concealed-crime/2014/05/09/id/570556/ Why live where the law requires that you be defenseless? In Detroit you can fight back, survive, and maybe even thrive eventually. You'll be like the Cossacks of Imperial Russia; independent warriors homesteading in the lawless borderlands. They'll write songs about you. http://www.bing.com/videos/search?q=song+a+country+boy+can+survive+youtube&FORM=VIRE1#view=detail&mid=24332E1A84ACDB2B2CE824332E1A84ACDB2B2CE8. There'll be plenty of black people there you can buy your dope from too.

At this point the only way to set up conditions for positive change in Baltimore and in other similarly afflicted cities is to use the Leftists' own play book against them. Pull a "Cloward and Piven" and collapse the system. http://en.wikipedia.org/wiki/Cloward%E2%80%93Piven_strategy. Once the population of Baltimore reaches 70% black, its economy will likely cease to function (if it has not already). It will lose its major financial houses and all its convention and tourist business. If I were a white policeman in Baltimore, I would leave as soon as practical, because it will not be long before the city will be broke and unable to pay the generous pension that you were promised. Join a police force somewhere else, soon. Years later, after Baltimore has collapsed and the Lefty government and their hood-rat minions have been much diminished in power and influence, you can move back and reclaim the city of your ancestors.

Yo Lord Bavarian

A Wannabe Thug tries to Get Whitey Got in the Hood

On Saturday morning, May 16, 2015, I was stocking Boss John's yogurt case when three hoodlums came into the store to buy doughnuts. At my age I suppose I look like I should be managing the place, but am not. The most outgoing hoodlum kept looking at me. Before they went up front to check out he walked over to the yogurt case, seven feet and a case cutter from me, with that look in his eye I was getting from local displaced hoodrats the Friday before the riots.

My impulse to grab the razor if attacked bothered me, so I stopped and checked the stock on my U-Boat [look it up in an equipment catalogue bro] and found the handle was loose, meaning I could pull the 30 pound five-foot, U-shaped pipe with steel cross slats, from the bed of the freight cart at will, and use it to break legs.

The wannabe thug looked at me with his three Bavarian crème doughnuts in their box clutched with the kind of care I only reserve for large willing breasts, and kicked the base plate of the yogurt case. If I had been the manager I would have tackled him right there, and let his buddies beat me to establish myself as a target while I methodically broke his fingers. However, I do not care about this yogurt case. It is not my concern. I am a grunt, and will not have someone else's property—even if that someone else is a nice elderly man who told me how much he appreciated me three days before—to be used to bait me into a situation that could put my very freedom at risk.

Of course, when I was a manager I did not have to go there because everything in the neighborhood knew I would. Tackle one crack head on the asphalt and chase the other one a half mile in your poorly knotted tie, and the punks gain an understanding that you are not to be trifled with. But I am retired, am not being compensated for this level of headache. Since I do not believe in right and wrong, but only reciprocal honor-based relationships, I decide to let it go. And if the manager on duty comes around and gets in a scuffle, I'll lay these hoodrats out for him, but not until they establish themselves as a threat to him, on video.

I am not a man that often looks at a violent situation and says to himself, "Yeah, I win this easy."

I have gotten my ass kicked too many times for bravado to find much purchase in what's left of my ego. [Try

losing 160 stick fights and see how arrogant you are.]
But I look at these guys and know that I break them,
every one of them—and quickly.

The punk keeps kicking the case and then looking at me
challengingly.

I cut in the new Chobani coconut yogurt.

Bait not taken; no disastrous social/legal hook
imbedded in my mouth, he and his bitchez with dickez
leave.

I have remained outside The Boned Zone.

If I had said anything I might as well have painted a
bull's eye on my back. These kids have brothers,
uncles—fathers who are younger than I, mothers with
jobs who vote...

I might as well have been a black janitor 60 years ago
being picked on by rich white kids, or the black
dishwasher 20 years ago, who was stomped to death by
two white kids [who I knew and hated] in the mid
1990s on Key Highway in South Baltimore.

If you live or work in an African American Ethical Zone,
and you are white, you will be baited. Don't bite; there is
nothing to be gained and much to be lost.

Looting Harm City

How Many Patrons of A Mixed Race Baltimore Bar Bought Stolen Goods After the Riots?

As a grocer I was a combatants and officer in a war against shoplifters who stole from grocery stores for resale at bars and on buses and hair salons, the three favorite venues for the purveyors of stolen goods in Harm City. I now find myself socializing once or twice a week with middle aged people of various races and occupations, most of whom have habitually purchased stolen goods as we chat. However, in the wake of the nasty looting binge of a riot that all of these people vociferously condemned as we sat together at that very bar gazing at the burning cop cars, how many of them have purchased stolen goods at the bar?

Granted, only one of the seven venders admitted to be selling goods looted during the riots. However, if a citizen of a city is willing to purchase stolen goods, how can he expect his city not to be looted at the first opportunity by its 60,000 heroin addicts and 210 street gangs?

The Boned Zone

Below is a list of patrons, by occupation, who bought stolen goods. The bold listings at the bottom indicate those who declined.

White

4 barmaids

4 retail clerks

1 barber

1 sedan driver

1 laborer

1 pawn shop clerk

1 street artist

3 house wives

1 crack whore

1 traditional bar whore

3 construction workers

1 mechanic

The Boned Zone

2 painters

1 landscaper

2 men, occupation unknown

1 retired fireman

1 active military

1 government employee

1 writer

3 gay professional men

29 of 33 whites support looting, to 4 against—and, no, Adam, I am not one of the gay guys, but the writer.

Brown

1 newspaper delivery man

1 smoking hot mixed race babe, who likes white dudes with money, occupation unnecessary

2 of 2 Hispanics support looting

The Boned Zone

Black

4 postal workers

1 cook

1 teacher

1 principal

1 retired cop

1 cabbie

1 elementary school principal

1 drug dealer

4 females, employment unknown

2 hair dressers

1 street vender

1 nurse

1 waitress

1 sub shop clerk

1 accountant

The Boned Zone

1 financial consultant

1 pipefitter

4 men, employment unknown

1 traditional bar whore

1 oversexed slut who has banged all of the postal workers and treats them like discarded tires

2 ladies who like to shoot pool

1 retired railroad inspector and Vietnam vet

32 blacks out of 33 support looting, with one against

Overall

62 of 67 patrons of the mixed race sports bar support looting via word and action, while 5 do not.

What this number means, is that 93% of my employed and retired neighborhood adult acquaintances, who— except for the scrupulously honest drug dealer—believe themselves to be law abiding residents of Baltimore, support, by action and word, the burning of Laporsha Lawson's home, which she barely had time to carry her severely disabled son Khai'Lee from, as the Korean liquor store next to her house caught on fire and engulfed her every possession, including all of her son's medical equipment, at 1 a.m. April 28, at the very synchronized minute that five business in our neighborhood were looted.

When 93% of taxpaying citizens are willing to buy discounted liquor from a thug, the very week that two dozen liquor stores were looted, what does that say about the Baltimore ethos? A 7% decency rate among 30-60 year old home and vehicle buyers, makes one wonder what the numbers would be amongst teens and twenty-some things. No wonder the Maryland Jockey Club is talking about moving the Preakness to another Maryland venue.

Any decent conqueror of the ancient world would put us all to the sword on principal, and we'd deserve it.

Jeremy Bentham   May 19, 2015 8:23 PM EDT

"The rest of mankind who were not killed by these plagues still did not repent of the work of their hands; they did not stop worshiping demons, and idols of gold, silver, bronze, stone and wood—idols that cannot see or hear or walk. Nor did they repent of their murders, their magic arts, their sexual immorality or their thefts." - Revelation 9:20-21(NIV)

FYI: In the original Greek of the Book of Revelations the word used to describe "magic arts" or "sorcery" is "pharmakia", from which the English word "pharmacy", referring to the study of drugs and medicine, is derived. In ancient times making "magic" often involved the use of drugs and potions that gave one supernatural powers, such as the ability to foresee the future, talk to the spirits of the dead, win an athletic contest or make someone fall in love with you. Therefore, some modern biblical scholars have surmised that in the end times people will not only not repent of their murders, their sexual immorality and their thefts, but that they will also be unrepentant of their drug abuse.

Not that we intend to be preachy or judgmental or anything here. I'm just sharing some interesting trivia. Like Queen Elizabeth I, I am perfectly willing to let other people go to Hell in their own way.

The Sacred Animal

Return of Gang Rule In Baltimore

"The guides carry shotguns with triple 000 buckshot, very lethal at close range, grizzly bear are protected, it would be easier to murder one of my hunters than kill a sacred bear. Do Not, I repeat, Do Not try to take away the bull elk your hunter has shot the night before and was to dark to properly quarter the animal. Bears hear the gunshots and since they are protected it's like ringing the dinner bell, they know there is fresh meat on the ground. I say let the bastard have the meat. We will claim the antlers later. You become very skilled at tearing an elk down to load on the pack horses when a grizzly is popping his jaws just inside the tree line. My personal best was 20 minutes..."

-Ishmael

Ishmael is a reader who lives and hunts in the Rocky Mountains. He has been helping me with background material for a mountain main story. The funny thing is—and he has pointed this out—he has basically described a trip to the liquor store in West Baltimore, only the sacred, vicious, brown, protected predator is a two-leg, not a four-leg, as Black Elk would have said.

Now, if bears could figure out over a few generations that they are protected by the federal government, how long do you think it would take an urban youth who dreams of thugdom with his every rapping breath, to figure out that he now has the social status and legal leverage of the Baltimore Cops that held this city down with a reign of terror for 30 years?

The answer is, less than a week.

Since the riots working blacks have been staying away from work in droves—hundreds having lost their jobs and thousand having had hours cut due to the economic impact of the riots and purge—afraid of the new lords of the city, of what they will do with the power the police once had.

City homicides are up from 69 in 2014 to 96 during the same period this year.

West Baltimore has hosted 20 homicides so far this year, to 21 in all of last year.

We have had our 164th nonfatal shooting, up 60% from last year, while fatal shootings are only up 40%, which means turf wars with new unseasoned players in the line of fire.

In a blink of the media's disturbing eye Baltimore went back to the gory days of 1995, 20 years ago, when the drug gangs were taking over Baltimore and 1,000 homeowners per month fled the city. The salient difference is that Baltimore was then bringing in a hard ass New York cop to address the issues, where we now have a waffling bimbo mayor pulling the rug out from under her Uncle Tom police chief, and the police in full retreat, denying that they have any duty to protect anyone other than themselves—and who can blame them? A beaten force rarely takes time to save refugees as they retreat.

The days that made Baltimore worth writing about have returned, only my family is all now safely ensconced in the suburbs whence I evacuated them during the last race purge. Now I have a ringside seat, and a brawl is breaking out. We had three shootings last night and things are just beginning to get hot in the city.

I have long been critical of the war on drugs, as this federal initiative, enforced by local proxy police, has created a hardened and resourceful criminal class numbering between 2,000 and 5,000 strong in Baltimore. Once created by the oppressive campaign of police terror this many headed monster could only be made worse by one action, by calling back the police, by gutting BPD morale. This reminds me of another unjust, mismanaged, and gracelessly ended war, Vietnam, with the people of Baltimore now in the same position after the riots as the South Vietnamese were after that last U.S. helicopter got shoved into the sea.

I recall last year seeing a documentary about the reintroduction of wolves to Yellow Stone Park, and how they were wiping out the coyotes that had taken over their niche, with nary a Winchester packing human to keep them in check. Well, now that the BPD has stood down, and is no longer pulling security for weaker drug gangs, the stronger drug gangs who have felt the brunt of the BPD iron heel are coming back with a vengeance, a protected, sacred predator species reclaiming its place at the apex of the food chain.

It's a good day to be writer in Baltimore.

Riley   May 27, 2015 12:41 AM EDT

A Postscript,

I seldom comment on anything anywhere I see it on the web. In this case though, I had been checking out a new bourbon; 1792 Ridgemont Reserve, a Bardstown product at 93.7 proof. $28! I saw this piece and took some "offense" over being run off a kill. I believe this is a nonsense thread at this point, and there is only one thing of which I am certain:

1792 is great for starting discussions over obscure points with strangers.

'Good thing it's the web.

Live well...Riley

Riley   May 26, 2015 11:35 PM EDT

Ishmael,

You are involved in guided hunting and I am not. I am a novice compared to you fellows, and the problems I face are not yours. I abide by the law because "...to live outside the law you must be honest". I hunt only animals I am tagged for, and would never shoot a protected animal willy-nilly. But when the gun fires and the animal falls, man's law falls away for me and natural law takes over. This is sometimes an animal I have watched for days, and I am taking her on my own dirt. I am in no mood to back off, but probably would if it was a sow teaching her cub to raid. All things considered we have nothing to debate, except maybe calling black bears BOBO. They can be edgy. I already know how nasty the wildlife folks can be. Possibly more nasty than bears of any type.

Ishmael   May 22, 2015 9:00 AM EDT

Sorry Riley generally I would just leave this one alone, but here goes. If you get caught killing a grizzly in the wilderness you are arrested, you are subject to questioning by a federal agent of the Forest Service, if there are more than one of you they question u separated, making sure your story's are exactly the same. If you are lucky and have wounds to show they let you go, if not we'll grizzly are very expensive. I would lose my guide license forever. There are very few black bears in the wilderness the grizz eat them. We call black bears names like Bobo, Yogi, grizz have names like Conan the Destroyer, Grim Reaper, the Terminator, also assassin was a joke, ok and I'd rather eat young females any day too, more tender. Ishmael.

Riley   May 21, 2015 1:13 AM EDT

I have no knowledge of the fabled Grizzly. We have 9 black bears in my canyon, and they are aggressive when it comes to quarreling over a kill.

I just hunt and keep a weapon at hand, including a heavy handgun in the armpit. Bears flow like water over terrain we cannot handle so quickly that one may well be caught out, and I do not belittle them. Still, they can pop their jaws all they like. It's just a heads-up.

I just hunt. I do not think of myself as an assassin, rather a fellow who prefers fresh, un-doctored meat. The seasons change and the world revolves. The Elk are calving as we chatter, and the deer are amazing. I can think of no better way to pay for my sins than to go down fighting over my next meal. But remember, I am old.

Protected you say? I would shoot the bastard down in an instant and work out the details at my leisure. Of course, I would do the same thing in Baltimore. Sorry, that's why I live apart.

Ishmael   May 20, 2015 4:40 PM EDT

PS Riley the grizzly are "Protected" we cannot shoot until they latch on to one of us, that was the point. They have no fear and respect no man, kind of like the hood rats in Baltimore.

ishmael   May 20, 2015 4:32 PM EDT

Riley, they call me Ishmael, we did go back and recover the bull next morning. Problem was a large boar grizzly had claimed the elk for his own. One of the younger less experienced guides picked a fight with him,the bear charged and we almost became bear shit, I'm a paid assassin so I track down the animal that I am paid to do.I agree with you when it comes to hunting for myself, that is why I quit doing the job,I'm not a trophy hunter, have a lot more respect for a animal than most humans, but that's another story. The bear and I survived, if you really want to live and feel adrenaline rush piss off a grizzly.

Riley   May 19, 2015 8:26 PM EDT

James,

Again with the thanks for the continuing feed on the troubles. It is as though I am wealthy with a spy on the ground. The bear thing struck a chord, but was puzzling. When I go forth to kill my neighbors for meat I get tags for Doe Deer, Cow Elk and Bear. Always eat young females. Who needs some old thousand-point stringy bull? You can pick his rack up in a month or so anyway. I do not employ hunters, guides or beaters. I cannot fathom letting a bear eat an animal taken in fair chase. I go forth on my own to harvest my own land, and if a bear happens to come along I get a rug and a pile of greasy meat to boot. Be prepared always works.

Were I a churchy type of man I would pray for you in your chosen site. It seems to be sliding apart, and only so many paths will remain safe. I would find it hard to relax there. Still, it takes all types...and I'm starting to get your fiction.

Inchon John

A Profile of an Urban Blight Casualty

John is a tall, gentle man with a quite demeanor, from Inchon Korea, who has owned and operated a small beat up liquor store on the main drag in Hamilton for these past five years [or longer, as I have only lived here for five years]. John's only employee was a former lightweight boxer who stocked the cases and provided security. I've been a regular for the past couple years, and John has treated me no differently then his black customers. But beginning in September of 2014, with increased violent crime against Hamilton businesses, John had become edgy. Since February he has been treating me like the Korean liquor store owners used to treat me down in Gardenville—nothing gardenlike about it—in the 1990s.

The basic strategy—now adopted by the Sikh liquor store owner up the street as well—is to take the black customer first. Since all liquor store robbers are black, the proprietor hopes to discourage a stick up by arranging it to occur before a witness. This works well as black men and women are generally so into their king and queen complex that they savor the apparent favoritism. The liquor store owner then discounts the white man's cost for his trouble. John began doing this with me as he got ever more nervous. Then, when the riots hit, he would engage me in conversation after the transaction and thank me for visiting him.

John stopped bringing in stock when the riots hit, expressed grave misgivings about the lack of police protection after the riots, and has not brought any stock in for the past three weeks since the riots, shortening his hours more every week as he lost business.

John no longer opens his liquor store. I do not know why. Someone said he was having financial troubles.

'When the Cops Have Kicked Your Door In'

Billy's Cop-Thug Odyssey

Yesterday, proud of my output, and hoping to take credit for Jim Fry's output as well, before retiring to the nether reaches of my lopsided futon mattress on the slanted wooden floor above SJ's office, I sought refreshment at the mixed race sports bar, where I made Billy's acquaintance.

I have nodded to Billy, said hello, and even patted him on the back, but today I learned his name. He is a struggling white blues guitarist and music buff of 37 years, who looks much younger. As soon as he speaks through that John Lennon mouth you just know he has smoked pot on most of the days of his half done life.

Billy is a well read, intelligent, super nice guy, who, for some reason, has trouble with short term recall.

When the news came on at 5:00 it went right to a press conference, in which the police commissioner was being taken to task by reporters on behalf of neighborhood associations and church leaders of West Baltimore, who

The Boned Zone

claim that the predominantly black third of the city is now an un-policed crime zone—a veritable Wild West!

The chief responded, "Our officers are routinely surrounded by twenty, thirty people...video cameras and hostility...We have to send in multiple units just to do basic police work."

Billy pointed at the monitor and said, "Bullshit, he's lying, making that up."

Seeing as how he had my attention, Billy continued as I put pen to register receipt.

"I've been mugged, worked over, almost killed by a group of young guys [We are in a mixed race setting, so he uses his eyes to indicate that they were black.], just like most of the people that live in this area. My case was pretty bad. I was drunk to begin with, and didn't even remember the encounter until the next day. The people at Shock Trauma asked me what happened and I said, 'I fell,' and they were like, 'Oh, it was a lot more than that!' I had no skin on the right side of my face and had swelling of the brain. They said I would have died if my friend's father hadn't seen me lying on the sidewalk. It was down by Belvedere and Traymore, behind the Royal Farms store."

"I learned a lesson then, to never talk back to a group of young guys that mouth off at you. Just keep quiet and keep on going.

"The other lesson I learned was at the hands of this fine gentleman's organization, the stat-massaging goon squad that reports an attempted murder as a mugging, and doesn't go back and update a shooting to a murder after the poor guy dies in the hospital a week later.

"My girl and I were driving home from a gig one night. I had just moved into a new rental. When I pull up I see that the door had been knocked off its hinges and cops were hauling out my computer. Dude, I don't break any law more serious than smoking a joint. I figured this was a mistake, and it was. I asked the cops what's up and they say, 'Are you, Reggie Johnson?'

[Billy, does not look like Reggie Johnson—any Reggie Johnson. In fact, I challenge the people of America to find a Reggie Johnson who looks like a 25 year old John Lennon.]

"They're like, 'Reggie Johnson lives at this address, Can you prove you are not Reggie Johnson?"

"So, I show them my I.D. and neglect to keep my mouth shut. The only thing you should ever say until you see your lawyer is, 'Am I under arrest?' Everything else is asking for trouble.

"First of all, they acted like complete assholes; ruffed up my girl, coped a feel, pressed my face against something hard that I supposedly owned!

"Unfortunately, I had been caught speeding, ten miles over the limit, in a school zone at one a.m. at some point in the past. When I was pulled over they searched my car, and found my little brother's nun-chucks. So, on my record is a charge—not a conviction, because it was thrown out of court—for a 'concealed deadly weapon.' That was all she wrote. My girl and I spent the weekend in jail, just because I was renting an apartment where some criminal used to live.

"Could you imagine if I was black? Fuck that, I'll take white getting stomped by black youth to black getting worked over by Baltimore's finest any day of the inequitable week."

There you have it Boned Zone readers, from a man who knows, the two venues for Boned Zone encounters: minding your own business and getting jacked up by cops, or minding your own business and getting jacked up by black youth. There really is not another selection on the menu. For smelly bikers and middle aged black panthers you need to check on the special of the day page.

"With individual cops who do not come off as complete assholes right off the bat—which isn't many—humor does work. Tom and I were stumbling home one time, and we were so drunk we just fell over on the sidewalk. A cop pulled up and said, 'What's going on here?'

"I said, 'I've fallen, and I can't get up,' reaching for the First Alert button.

"The cop was cool. He said, 'Look, you guys are of age. How about I give you a lift home?' and he did. I suppose cops like that get eaten alive in West Baltimore."

'Fueling A Phony Sense of Oppression'

Feds To Sink 163 Million Dollars Into Inciting More Unrest in Baltimore

As it stands in Baltimore police work is excluded in one third of the city unless a tactical squad is on hand. Stay tuned as the balkanization of an American ghetto continues to enjoy federal support, even as the local politicians get thrown under the proverbial city bus by their nefarious masters.

This morning I was on the back of the #55 bus with a gang member, a senior thug of perhaps 25, heavily tattooed with tags, as he discussed his part as the liaison for an East Side gang, in working out West-East distribution. It's been 15 years since I listened to gangsters conduct business above a whisper on public transportation. I am pleased that the Chicago Mulatto has authorized subsidies for my favorite live action crime drama.

"Matthew Vadum, an expert in left-wing activist groups and the author of "Subversion, Inc.," warns such federal funding invariably finds its way into the hands of progressive activists who personally profit from increased community tensions."

- See more at: http://moonbattery.com/?p=58702#sthash.MP4CHsGH .dpuf

According to this webzine article federal funds that are supposedly being infused into Baltimore to build and repair relations between the police and disgruntled citizens, are instead being funneled to left wing riot organizers such as Al Sharpton. For more on the astonishing charge cited in the subtitle above click on the link below.

I personally think this is brilliant politics on the part of the White House, as local unrest can only strengthen the federal position.

http://moonbattery.com/?p=58702

Jeremy Bentham   May 21, 2015 7:27 PM EDT

Spot on analysis by Moonbattery! Whatever is wrong, you have to throw more tax money at the problem, don't you? That is The Woman's way. The Woman always needs federal money to create more cushy patronage jobs for her minions (especially as the tax base of the city disappears). If this follows the pattern of Chicago, expect to see gang leaders placed on the city payroll as special advisors, youth counselors, ministers without portfolio, or whatever. Now you know what the hidden agenda was, why the city government held the police back and let the rioters run wild. It's all a big extortion racket. Help we need money to fix the urban unrest! Historically Leftist agitators, both black and white, have always wanted more federal government control over the states and the major cities. Among other things they always believed that if the states were allowed to have their own way, they would bring back the "Jim Crow" laws. Especially former slave states like Maryland. At least that is what they have persuaded the black community at large to believe. But hey, the harassment and "murder" of black men by the police in Baltimore and elsewhere just proves that that really is a clear and present danger, doesn't it? Vote Democrat: we hate the people you hate and we'll punish them for you!

 **responds:** May 24, 2015 6:32 PM EDT

I now see the point of your 'Woman' construct for describing the political racket—it's just like being married to a gold digger who keeps insisting you adopt sons from inner city orphanages.

Jim Fry   May 21, 2015 6:34 PM EDT

Ding - I'll take "Update the Colloquialisms" for $2,000 on this daily double Alex!
A: "Follow the power, since it leads to the money."
Q: What is a more realistic version of the phrase "Follow the money.", given the politics in parlay?

'Four Minutes to Eleven'

Harm City Curfew Enforcement, In the Majority White Kane & Eastern Neighborhood, 2005

Valerie

Back when I was fourteen we had this eleven o'clock curfew for minors in our area, because it was supposed to be a bad area. I had some babysitting money and wanted to go buy some candy at the corner store, which was one and a half blocks away. It was like three minutes each way, so my mother let me leave at ten of.

I got to the store in a hurry and there was nobody in line, so I was out of there with four minutes to spare and heading home. As soon as I get out onto the sidewalk a cop rolls up and tells me I'm violating the curfew. I said, "Nahah, I got four minutes and just live around the corner."

He told me that I could not get home in four minutes and he was holding me for breaking the curfew and it wasn't even in force yet. But I was only breaking the curfew because he held me. I had the receipt to prove what time I left the store.

He wanted to search me but couldn't touch me without a female officer. He called for a female officer and no one showed up. I could have been home five times by the time he decided to have me search myself!

He had me empty out my purse, and sure enough, all I had was chips and candy. Then he had me take off my shoes—new Nikes I had just bought with my own money—and he ripped the soles out!

Then he told me to get in the back of the car, that he was driving me home, which he did, but I was locked in back there and my mother got really pissed thinking that I had been out there goofing around doing something stupid.

It was really ridiculous if you ask me.

Partay Central

The New Holiday Reality in Harm City

On Memorial Day evening I stopped by a friend's house in the Cedonia area about three miles to my east. I had been out in Harford County with family for the holiday. What I saw in the majority black working class area of Cedonia was interesting, in that police were not visible and men were drinking in the streets and on sidewalks. On the way home I was actually frightened by some of the characters I saw skulking about just as darkness fell.

Hookers were openly doing business in a gas station parking lot.

Groups of teens and young men were gathered in alleys keeping an eye on people walking up the side streets. Each one of these groups had a single bicyclist mounted on a BMX style bike. I was followed twice and then, when I was seen to be aware, as I stopped every half block and locked all around, the youths tracking me broke off and returned by the way they had come.

Cookie told me that on Sunday Night she had difficulty driving on a busy secondary street that was so packed with double parked cars and people drinking and dancing [this normally requires a block party permit] that it took her many hair raising minutes to travel a few blocks. She said that the partygoers were generally genial and did not harass the whites. The fascinating aspect was the lack of a police presence. It seems like the New York brand of lifestyle policing [arresting for loitering, open container and lack of I.D.] imported into Baltimore by the New York cop [Norris]often credited with reducing crime in Baltimore, has gone the way of Rome.

In the past week the Baltimore Police Commissioner has held at least one news conference for local news only—no doubt under political pressure to get Baltimore out of the headlines—and an anonymous city cop has given CNN an interview, indicating that the morale has never been lower.

Also, the none fatal shooting rate has increased another 6%, now standing at 66% more than 2014. Arrests continue to drop and crime continues to increase, particularly black-on-black gang violence.

Although the city administration has tried to depict the violence surge in Baltimore as confined to the West Side, specifically the area of the riots, the increase in violent crime has been citywide, just as the unreported purge attacks during the riots occurred across a broad geographic area.

The number of males exhibiting a desire to engage in opportunistic aggression is greatly increased. Moving quickly, and in a state of awareness, is of paramount importance in such environments.

AVD Combatives

Methods for Defending an Alternative Speaking Venue

Note: When I write gouge I mean rake. For low impact, low energy, minimal physical risk unarmed combatives nothing beats poking or scraping the eye. So when I write gouge I don't suggest digging that thing out of the socket, but just scratching the cornea or shocking the eye muscle or tear duct to render an intruder ineffective.

This article discusses Asymmetrical Venue Defense methods. News film clips viewed through the YouTube window at the base of the article may be used as a tactical study. This is a film of two dozen aggressors pushing one man out of a speaking venue. The question is, how could three to five able defenders protect this man and keep him at his podium, with three being all you can jam into a car with this guy, and five most likely the maximum number that could be gathered from a gym or martial arts club on short notice.

Positions

1. Bodyguard, the man dedicated to the subject's defense, someone who can drop bodies with his empty hands and is cool enough to use an improvised weapon without going ape shit and killing someone.

2. Doorman, the man who defends access to the venue, a big, big dude, ideally a wrestler or offensive lineman. Wing Chun or aikido experience would be a huge benefit.

3. Tactician, the rover who scouts for and reinforces the other two, basically the same profile as the bodyguard, but more ruthless.

4. [Optional] second doorman

5. [Optional] second tactician stationed outside the venue with a communication link to the lead man on his tactical team, who will hit intruders from behind.

The tactics used by this group of 'louts' below consists of posing, pacing, pushing—three faces of aggression.

Asymmetrical defenses are preferred, using large staff against small intruders, small staff against large intruders, grappling versus striking, striking versus grappling, with small joint manipulation, foot stomping and eye gouging as the default tactics. Ideally your super heavyweight doorman breaks the feet of the small men and the fingers of the large men, with the tactical man commanding compliance or dishing out KOs of those who get past the doorman, and the bodyguard ruthlessly disposing of anyone who touches the primary. To keep up appearances, women who touch the primary should only have their feet broken—one foot will suffice. Our men should not be seen touching women with their hands.

Contact Priorities

1. The doorman is not to attempt to deny access to such a large body, but rather tax them and let them pass one at a time. I'm thinking of Cory here, our 6 and a half foot tall 370 pounder, who practices breaking feet. Once he's at the bottom of a pile he is useless. His priority is to stay on his feet and, as each person manages to squeeze by, breaking a thumb, and stomping on a foot. He should wear heavy engineer boots, and keep his chin tucked against punches that might come. No matter what, the doorman does not throw punches. Cory, let them through the door as soon as you have broken a finger or a foot. With large intruders a thumb lock while using a literal ankle press might be necessary. Do not push back

but through. Big men who push should be pushed past you and tripped, for the tactical man to disable while they are on the deck.

2. The tactical man [I'm thinking myself here] first instructs peaceful attendees that at the first sign or trouble, they are to retreat to the walls and keep clear of the common space. If this is an open venue with no movable seating equipment than this man needs to come armed with the largest flashlight available, for making certain that the subject might be escorted through a darkened venue if the lighting is compromised. If the door is breached than any male intruder with a face mask is to be hammered in the jaw with the flashlight and KO'd. If this is a venue with movable seating, then the flashlight is handed off to the bodyguard. Bar stools and folding chairs make ideal pole axes for breaking legs. Any male intruder should have his leg pole-axed.

3. The bodyguard [I'm thinking Oliver or Craig] will need to deal with people who attempt to touch the subject. Ideally this guy is a boxer. Men must be dropped as soon as they near the subject, with chin shoots preferred. Aggressively dangerous women should just have their ankle stomped until useless, with one inside stomp probably all that is needed. If the tactical flashlight has been handed off to the bodyguard

this should be used alternately to jab the body and smash the jaws of male intruders.

Note: Females who link arms are not capable of stopping or harming the speaker or pushing him out of the venue, so cut out the males who link with them by breaking their fingers and thumbs through unobtrusive small joint manipulation.

Overall, the defenders should use the following action cue scale:

1. Deny access to intruders

2. Compromise the ability of aggressive intruders by breaking hand and foot bones in an unobtrusive and subtle way, and push tripping them face first through the door rather than going down with them.

3. Disable aggressive intruders that have entered the venue and are advancing on the speaker's personal space.

4. Intruders who enter and do not advance on the speaker must be commanded to take off their masks and kneel.

5. Once all intruders are disabled or compliantly kneeling, their shoestrings should be tied together.

6. Any member of the security team who is injured or struck, or successfully immobilized [or any member who sees this happen to another member] should shout breach, which is the cue to blind intruders with eye jabs, spear hands, and gouging attacks, until an intruder rout has been achieved.

7. An egress point separate from the entrance way must be established by the team immediately upon arrival, and should be the way by which the subject is ushered from the venue if there is a breach.

8. The bodyguard is never to leave the personal space of the subject, even to aid a team member. No able bodied male must be permitted in the personal space of the subject, personal space being defined as within arm's length. I kind of like the idea of cutting out the men and letting the short women ring the tall Aryan speaker like his sexual property on display.

If possible choose a private venue with choke points and poor visibility, such as a bar, where the owner will take part in the defense arrangements, as opposed to hotels or restaurants whose staff and management have a passive orientation toward intruders.

As American society continues to devolve into a kind of caricature of 1920s Germany, I see an increased level of government tolerance extended to leftist groups who wish to attack free speakers, and suggest seeking privately secured speaking venues and bringing a security team, rather than trusting to speaking venues typically used by the elite and media.

Private security firms that are not completely useless are rare and expensive. In dire circumstances, such as being targeted by violent groups, the only organizations capable of providing effective security will be sports teams and gangs. Police forces are no longer a threat to violent actors, with the possible exception of those defending your venue. Legal defensibility will need to be a guiding principal in your arrangements, with any weapons in the hands of the security team being a gross liability.

For someone such as Jared Taylor, asking a local rugby, boxing, wrestling, or MMA team to provide security at a barroom setting would be ideal for dealing with college hoodlums. Even during the Baltimore Riots the only venues that rioters were prevented from entering were barrooms protected by one or two athletes, who the rioters avoided like the plague even as they attacked police! A study of the body language and physical make up of these college age groups indicates close to zero combat effectiveness. Two dangerous men could take one of these groups apart. Part of the effectiveness of these groups is that they rely on the civility of their victims. This is another reason to choose a bar as a speaking venue as the police tolerate a certain level of violence at drinking establishments and come to the door assuming that the bouncer was justified in taking out a rowdy intrusive element. I highly recommend that intellectuals such as Taylor seek the safety of a biker bar.

For more on this subject check out

'Are The Counter-Currents People Cowards?'

Tactically Speaking

While the article you have just read is based on my thoughts as a security lead for a venue such as that filmed below—which was a disastrous goat fuck from the get go—Tactically Speaking stresses venue selection and minimizing legal liabilities, so comes off differently.

Militant Devolution

Note that the very non athletic attackers armed with hammers in this video would not only justify the use of chairs—even for head shots—but make easy meat for such tactics as well. I'm over fifty and I'll pit myself with a chair against four of these jokers and pick the old man for an easy win.

https://www.youtube.com/watch?v=Iz3BuqTQdMc

Kman   May 30, 2015 1:00 PM EDT

Incidents like this are much more likely in places where people are unable to bear arms and where use of force laws favor the criminals. Where I live, Mr. LaFond's methods might expose the defenders to legal liabilities. Use of intermediate force weapons such as chemical sprays and hand help electronic stun guns leave little to no physical injuries. Hand held stunners might be particularly useful in a melee of unarmed lefties such as Mr. Jared encountered

responds: June 1, 2015 1:59 PM EDT

Your insights are correct, in my view, Kman.

I did see footage of some cops using pepper spray during the riots and it necessitated them leaving the formation, and had some effect against police and reporters [sob, sob] when the wind shifted, and could affect bystanders in doors.

I think hand held stunners would be a great weapon in such a melee situation. The problem with stunning devices is that a falling body's head can hit hard objects. Just last year a hospital 4 miles from where I sit saw a young man killed by a police stun device in the ER! So, although there will be less aggregate injury from stun devices compared to impact weapons, there will still be injury.

Also, my recommendations in this scenario are, I believe, at the extremity; the outer limits of what I perceive as legally defensible. I've taken other, milder, stances in some of the attached articles.

That said, if I'm protecting someone like Mr. Jared, and some big meathead puts his hands on him, then said meathead is hitting the deck hard. This is one reason why I have almost always refused to work such situations, because of where it could go.

The more I have thought about it the more I recommend using biker bars as speaking venues. It also seems from some of the Bowden footage, and inferences he has made as to other un filmed venues, that he choose drinking establishments and club type facilities, over open hotel rooms and university venues that would favor leftist force, but local venues integrated into the community that would favor the right.

You are definitely right about some of my recommended methods being legally problematic, which, no matter the municipality, is always the reality when a small group defends against a large group, aggravated by the fact that law enforcement focuses on results rather than the actual initial act of aggression, generally placing blame squarely on the shoulders of any successful defender.

Thanks for expanding the discussion.

'Who Doesn't Matter'

Harm City One Month After The Purge

No matter the society, it has never been an outrage to kill, only to kill certain people. In ancient Sumer killing a slave was frowned upon, but not an outrage. In 1820, killing Tasmanians was the thing to do. But kill a British naval officer and there was hell to pay. The high priests of our media church have now decided that people who were recently killed without outcry are now martyrs, and that people who were once treasured by a community, are no longer taboo victims.

The thing about being in The Boned Zone that really sucks, is that you know that society does not care. Your attackers have come for you knowing this, knowing that you have no right to defend yourself, that you represent the guilt of your savage ancestors, that you will not be mourned by your money grubbing masters, and that your slack-eyed peers will blame you for choosing to be where you should not have been.

The Boned Zone

A full 30 days after the so called Baltimore Riots, bus use is still at 50% of normal. Bus drivers no longer attempt to enforce MTA regulations after dark. Young black men who do not wish to pay their fare are left alone. Of the various police departments humiliated a moon ago none was laid so low as the Maryland Transit Authority police. [The van burning on the main page of this site was one of theirs.]

Arrests are down in the city, way down, with one exception, whites are being arrested as often as usual. At this point that is just an assertion of mine based on speaking with a handful of cops, criminals, witnesses and victims. I wonder if the racial arrest numbers for this month will come to light.

I, myself have been jumpier than I had been before the purge. Last night, as I walked past the 7-11, I heard the scuff of a shoe behind me and turned to confront the person, where before I would have glided off to the right and let him pass. He backed up, walked around, and walked by me in the street. We were both still feeling the edge from being hunted so blatantly last month.

On the bus home this morning it was nearly deserted, only one student going to school instead of a dozen in the county. No students in the city, out of two dozen that usually take that line. Some of this is end of school year attendance fall off. Not all of it.

A man was standing over me waiting for a seat when I woke. I made to move over and he said, "No, no, no, Sir," pointing to a lady that was leaving, indicating that he would take her seat. The last time I remember adult males being this courteous and jumpy was in the early 1990s when the drug war was kicking into high gear and men seemed to call a truce across racial lines as we all looked out for the teens with the guns and the 20 pair of man stomping sneakers.

A sense of danger has its upside; solitude as people choose to leave their homes less often, and aggressive courtesy among men across racial divides. Two days ago I stopped at a gas station to get a drink, and waited patiently behind a black man who was buying over $100 worth of lottery tickets with specific numbers. I settled in for my 10 minute wait. The Pakistani attendant, in the time before the purge, would have said to the lottery customer, "One minute, sir, while I take care of him."

No such customer service choice would be risked in our new African American Ethical Zone. The man was my age or older. When he realized what was going on, he took the initiative to set things straight, telling the clerk, "Please, take this man before you finish with me."

He seemed genuinely embarrassed that the clerk was afraid of him.

The clerk used the next 20 seconds making the transaction—twenty seconds that could have gotten him beaten to death if that were a young black man rather than a mature black man in front of me. I thanked the man and he wished me a good day. I am coming to like this lawlessness, this knowledge that the police will not come when called, or, if they do, will hold back from enforcing the law upon the majority. The animals are showing themselves for what they are, and the cops for the crutches of state they are. Men are learning to be men again, practicing courtesy and making tactical decisions, not leaving their fate in the hands off the State at every turn.

There is a new life value system in Baltimore. If a Baltimorean is slain, he will only be mourned by the national media priesthood **if** he is a black male slain by a white male or a law officer.

The local media priesthood will also mourn black males slain by other black males, and white women or children who are slain by anyone.

The Boned Zone

Of the 38 people who have been murdered so far this month—making this the most violent month since 1996—the two most recent were a young mother and her seven year old son, killed in the Uplands neighborhood of West Baltimore, in their home. Not being warriors in this undeclared race war, these two humans have no value to their oppressed community, and will be mourned in a very limited way. There will be no national media outcry on behalf of this baby. Neighbors who saw the killers come and go will not give statements to the police.

http://www.nydailynews.com/news/crime/baltimore-boy-8-murdered-city-bloody-continues-article-1.2238941

I live in a city where thugs beaten and killed by cops are worshipped as martyrs, and women and babies murdered in their bed by thugs do not rate a media tear.

And somehow, it feels right, like this is the real Baltimore, the nation's seeping cold sore, a pox on the body politic; oozing its toxic puss in the form of its negligent mayor asking FEMA for a 20 million dollar bailout and telling reporters they are "out of line," for asking her about the crime surge that followed the race purge. It is refreshing to find that Tyranny can still be such an empty-headed slut.

http://www.foxnews.com/us/2015/05/29/murder-capital-baltimores-homicide-explosion-in-wake-freddie-gray-case-dwarfs/

hillcountry   May 29, 2015 11:29 PM EDT

howdy James,

think you'll find this interesting reading

https://www.traditionalright.com/victoria/

'Stuck on Stupid'

Raphael Among The Dominicans

Oliver and I ran into Raphael at the gym last night. He was irritated about something recent in his personal life. As always it was not difficult to draw the incident out of him.

"I'm at the barber shop last night—where I watch the fights with my Dominican friends and we shoot the breeze. For some reason—either because I'm the only Puerto Rican there, or the oldest, or the smallest, this one dumbass drunk Dominican starts with me.

"Juan is saying, 'Oh Poppy he wants some!'

"The other guys are like, 'Do not mess with him,' meaning for this fool not to mess with me.

"The one thing I can't stand about Dominicans is the way they approach you when they want to start something, like this [half squats, leans, and hangs head down while pawing with the open hand]. This fool keeps on saying, in Spanish, 'Don't you understand me?'

"Well, I had enough. This guy was stuck on stupid. So I stepped away and he steps after me and—Bam! I kicked him in the groin, heel kicked his balls in. He grabbed himself and leaned forward so I slapped him across the face and he went down.

"The guys in the barber shop are all laughing, pointing to my [Wing Chun instructor] card, and saying, 'Hey Raphy, can you teach me some of that?'

"I was like, 'That was no martial art—that was nothing. This fool was stuck on stupid so I just got him off that stupid spot.'

"Then Juan comes up to kick this guy—because he hates this guy—and I say, 'No. it's done. Take him to the bathroom in case he shits himself,' and he dragged him away.

"It's getting crazy out there brother—the wild west. The cops don't come when you call anymore. They show up at the ER where I work to collect the bodies, but don't expect to see them on the street."

Combat Notes

Raphael was certain of successfully dropping his antagonist when he stepped away and the man followed. As in boxing, walking your man into something is a good finishing gambit.

On a more technical note, although he claimed the kick was not 'art' it was clearly an inside stomp kick of the Wing Chun variety [Benson Henderson has used this in the octagon to the body.] with the heel delivery causing the testicles more pain as they were smashed against the leg or pelvis. The thing with groin strikes is to drive the balls into the pelvis.

The slap instead of a punch, and the preventing of Juan from 'piling on,' increased Raphael's odds of defending against any criminal or civil case that might be brought against him, and will also limit his antagonist's thirst for revenge, which is something to consider, particularly in an open city.

The Blue Flu

Police Response Anecdotes from the Last Week of May, 2015

The Baltimore Sun—seemingly a newspaper again—is reporting that the medical centers and pharmacies that were looted last month have still not been visited by the police. These companies have video surveillance of men and women using crow bars to pillage safes, ATMs, drug lockers, etc., and the Baltimore PD will not even send a detective to look at the tapes.

Over 300 businesses have filed insurance claims.

Over 50 businesses have closed.

Of 159 fires set it is unclear how many have been investigated.

Demoralized by the mayor who told them to let the city they are charged with defending burn, and afraid to confront blacks for fear of mob violence and DOJ reprisals, the BPD is essentially on strike. It will be interesting to see where this leads as Baltimore-based criminals adapt to an un-policed environment.

Interracial violence by blacks—which is to say all interracial violence—is still not close to the black on black crime rate, with all of the months 30-plus murders suspected of being black on black.

If that changes will whites still sit on their soft hands and whine?

Miss Ezz

"It's getting scary out here. I've been having nightmares about coming to work, afraid I'll get mugged or beaten up. The overtime cop didn't show up for work today, and the police department no longer answers the overtime phone on weekends."

Allain

[One of the last white sedan drivers in Baltimore City]

"I went to leave for work on Monday and, when I get to the front door, I see these three guys breaking into my car—they were albino Eskimos, of course. I stand right there at my door and call nine-one-one, speak with the operator, and describe these guys, what they are doing to my car, and ask them to send someone out. She keeps me on the phone until they're done—didn't get anything but change—mostly just damaged the windows. The pigs show up two days later and ask what's up!"

Mystique

"I was sitting at the McDonalds on White and Belair watching this dude punch the shit out of this girl. The funny thing was, two cops were sitting there watching it too. When 'Dude' was done beating her face in the cops lost interest and drove off.

Leroy

"The cops didn't come when I called about these hoodlums. Thanks to this dumb bitch mayor I can't even sit on my stoop anymore. Not one of those hoodlums is getting prosecuted for the twenty cops they put in the hospital, so why should I expect the cops to help me out, especially with that dummy not backing them up? Shoot, it ain't even hot out here at night yet. Wait 'til these niggers start to sweat!"

The Deadliest Month

With 43 Harm Citizens Slain, The Baltimore Sun Reviews Harm City's Lethal History

Observations on the June 1, 2015 front page article **May was deadliest month in 40 years** by Mark Puente of The Baltimore Sun

As the Mulattress-in-Chief notes that 189 of the 208 Baltimoreans killed in 2014 were black men, and calls for a stop to "the killing of African American men," the families of the politically un-mourned black women and children, and the unwanted whites among us might take her statement as an admittance of culpability.

Up until the Race Purge of late April 2015, the Baltimore Police Department had three core tasks.

#1 was fighting the drug war against black gangs, which in effect meant that the police were acting as a "God Gang" beating up and dismantling the top black gangs, and thus taking heat off of the lesser black gangs.

#2 was fighting the drug war by arresting drug users, as likely to be white as black

#3 was protecting businesses

At the height of the purge, triggered by the death of a drug gang member at the hands of the police, the mayor announced that business would not be protected. Now, with the police being investigated by the DOJ for their zealous commitment to the DEA drug war, what is there left for them to do?

Businesses are no longer the concern of the police.

Drug gangs are now sacred cows of inequity to be let range the transmigrant narco state.

During the purge the police announced that they could not, and would not, defend citizens and were good to their word. So now that the "protect and serve" myth has been unmasked, what are the police to do? The police are even declining to investigate property crimes against major businesses.

The police merely remain on station as the municipal government's civic guard, to hold media venues and government facilities against the rampaging hordes when another purge is declared by the gangs.

The Boned Zone

According to the mayor the only civic priority seems to be protecting the lives of black men, who make up the same vast proportion of victims, murderers, rioters, and purge troopers. This makes as much sense as the U.S. going into an Islamic nation to protect Muslims from Muslims.

In any case, as the ineptitude rolls on here are some numbers dredged up by The Baltimore Sun, which has suddenly been called upon to be a newspaper again.

Baltimore Homicide Sampler

Bracketed notes are mine.

2015, to date: 116 homicides

May 2015 homicide rate per 100,000 population: 6.1

May 2015: 43 homicides [heroin & crack turf wars]

August 1990: 42 homicides [crack & heroin turf wars]

August 1972: 45 homicides [heroin turf wars]

December 1971: 44 homicides [heroin turf wars]

Observations

1. The high killing in 1971-72 came with the ramping of the heroin trade, and in the wake of recent unrest in the form of the 68 riots.

2. I infer from [1.] that we are just seeing the tip of the iceberg as far as the effect on local crime patterns stemming from the defeat and emasculation of the Baltimore Police Department in the recent purge.

3. As indicated by the lethal shooting distribution outside of West Baltimore, and the three men shoot to death in Eastside shootings on Sunday, the mayoral and police brass focus on West Baltimore is propagandistic and meant to deflect the reality that upscale Eastside enclaves are now beleaguered communities, and will be hit the hardest in the next purge. 4. August

Ishmael   June 1, 2015 4:49 PM EDT

Where's Robo Cop when you need him.

responds: June 2, 2015 11:39 PM EDT

Hopefully getting refitted!

Big Chev versus 'the Tough Guy'

An Epic Stockroom Brawl: A Sketch on Skirting The Boned Zone

The Boned Zone is that place where you are physically threatened by an antagonist and the entire society that makes a claim to your body and soul. The deeply disturbing and dichotomous nature of The Boned Zone, is that the more successful you are dealing with your antagonist's attempt to bone you, the more likely it is that you will get boned by the rest of the assholes on the planet who lay claim to the slice of it you happen to be treading on.

Big Chev is a husky Polish-American machinist who used to work at the store where I now find myself employed. I recall that when I took a part time gig at this location some 21 years ago that there had been a rumor that he had fought a coworker. Even though this guy was bleeding from a head wound Big Chev was not fired. The manager even warned me not to cross him when I was hired. I just became his best little buddy, like an evil version of The Skipper and Gilligan. After all these years, this past Tuesday, when the big man came into buy his breakfast, and checked on the genius twerp that was his favorite sidekick, that guy finally asked him about the fracas.

Big Chev on 'Breaking Bone Racks'

"Oh that, the tough guy in produce. I'm no world beater, but I don't go easy. I wouldn't live where you live, with all the monkeys 'cause I know the numbers would overwhelm me. You can only wring the necks of so many monkeys and chimps and baboons before you run into a gorilla or two and end up on the shit end of the deal.

"Anyhow, this guy was tall, thin, the longhaired hippie type, just out of prison—talked about fighting a lot and talked up the prison thing. That's how much of a loser he was—was proud of prison. We're both in our early twenties. This guy has never held a job for more than a month, and me, this is my job—my life. I get fired and I'm on the street—got bills, car, rent. So I never consider fighting on the job. I'll invite you to a meeting on the parking lot after hours, but that's as far as it goes.

"I'm on the dock checking in an order while the Fag receiver is doing God only knows what. And Tough Guy tells me to go tell Fruit Cake to come back on the dock.

I said, "You don't tell me what to do, pal."

He says, "You better watch how you talk to me big boy. I've been in prison—fought my ass off behind bars."

I say something like, "More like you tried to fight the monkeys off in prison and they fucked you in the ass from behind bars!"

"At this point I'm just walking off, not even looking at him, and he decided to wing me—a cheap shot."

Author's comment: "You mean he actually punched that polish cinderblock that's sitting on your neckless shoulders?"

"I never said he was bright. Just a little mousey ding he gives me. I barely felt it. But you're not just going to clip me on the job and get away with it. On the other hand, all I thought about the entire time after he started mouthing off to me was my job, that I didn't want to do anything to lose my job and end up like some pathetic loser on the street. So, in my mind, I'm not thinking fight. This is not a fight. If this was a fight this joker would be waiting for the ambulance.

"I turned and grabbed him and we got to a kind of wrestling situation and he's trying to hit me. Now if he hits me again I might get mad, and if I get mad, I might lose my job, and if I lose my job and get real mad, I might have to spend the next ten years ripping apart niggers in prison, and I'd rather rip apart spare ribs at the bar. So I grabbed him by the shoulders and slammed him against the forklift and blood squirted everywhere. This dude was definitely a bleeder. We've barely got started and this guy's already a bloody mess. I'm standing over him holding him with one hand, knowing that I could kill him with my bare hands, and all I could think about was my job. I was here to work, not to fight.

"I even helped this joker up—and then he shakes his head as Fruit Cake is coming back on the dock with his 'Hey guys, now, now,' routine, and the blood splashes across Fruit Cake's eyes!"

[Deep laughter]

"I wouldn't call it a fight. It was an altercation. But if some nigger or other kind of monkey ever lays a hand on me I sure hope there is forklift around!"

In most cases, under most employers, both of these guys are fired on the spot. Fortunately since Tough Guy and Big Chev shook hands, agreed that they had not been in a fight, and especially the fact that Tough Guy manned up and declined to go for medical treatment [which would have drawn a Workman's Compensation Investigation] they were both able to keep their jobs.

Today

In today's world situations like this are much less common, and the work place law suit has become such an institution, that if such a situation does arise both antagonists are likely to be boned by the greater society.

If you do find yourself responding impulsively to a sucker punch attack here are a few tips to help minimize the chance that the law or an avenger might come after you:

1. Do not punch back, but use asymmetrical counter measures so that the situation continues to look like an attack rather than a fight. Most eye witnesses never see the initial attack, but the second stage, which is your response, which might just look like an attack to someone who just turned their head.

2. Do not finish the guy or go into overkill, but back off when you have him at your mercy.

3. Do not let this be misunderstood as backing out. Stay there and either help him with his injuries, pat him on the back and say no hard feelings, or even extend your hand to help him up and offer to call it a draw, an accident, or whatever seems likely to work with this guy.

4. Making friends with him is a good idea. He is not in a position to make the overture without looking like a bitch, so that is your call.

As it is, verbal escalation to a brawl is exceedingly rare compared to criminal attacks. There is no sense in taking such a situation into overkill and possibly placing yourself as the target of a vengeful antagonist [the common comeback after a fight now is a stabbing by the loser, at a rate of about one per week in Baltimore County.] You also want to do what you can to stay out of the criminal clutches of law enforcement.

'The Survival Slide'

The Most Important Basic Combat Move for Urban Survival

The scenario occurs in The Boned Zone, that place where you are in physical, psychological and legal jeopardy, with some subhuman attacking you unannounced. This occurs either because you suffer from what noted Urban Philosopher T. Spoone Slickens termed Stupid White People Syndrome, and are speaking with this knucklehead, or, because you were unaware and he just walked up on you.

In survival situations, where a weapon is assumed and warnings will be as slim as the attacker can manage, I prefer using a stick-fighting model. The knife is too specific and the stick does generalize to the knife. Boxing is too ritualistic. You want the tools and techniques of the boxer and the knife fighter. But you want to move like a stick fighter.

In boxing and knife fighting one uses generally short steps to access the opponent's weak side. The knifer wants to jam the blade into the heart of his unarmed target while he avoids the strong hand. The boxer usually prefers not to move into his opponent's rear right hand and thus walk into a power punch.

In stick fighting—and also in blade dueling—it is a common and sound strategy to move to your left and his right, ideally as his weapon passes, so that you are behind his forehand striking arc and away from the pesky empty hand that just might grab your stick or trap your knife hand.

Dealing with knife, club, rock, bottle, and fist wielding aggressors is more like dealing with a moderately skilled stick-fighter than a boxer or knife duelist.

The vast majority of your potential attackers break down like so:

1. The Bum-rusher who will shove you, often to knock you down so that others might stomp you. These tend to push off with the rear right foot.

2. The Goon who grabs you with his left hand and beat you with their right

3. The Runt who might shoot in for the waist-tackle, straight away or after a chest shove

4. The Sucker Puncher who will wing away with the right, most likely while you are not focused on them— so the punch is already hitting or missing when you first perceive it

5. The Sucker Clubber behaves identically to the sucker puncher

6. The Knifer, the most dangerous and common of which holds the knife back in a rear right hand and pitches the point into your torso as he uses his left hand to check or grab you depending on his need.

All of these aggressors bring their energy from the right. Therefore you want to go right as that will put you outside of his wheel house, his pocket. In weapon fighting we call that a pass. You want to pass his weapon so that you can come in behind it, or keep going.

Against a bum-rusher or waist-tackler stepping offline either way is good. So you might as well step right because the two nastiest guys, the goon and the knifer, want to grab you with their left hand and then murder you with their right. Deny them the first part of their attack and make them reach out with the rear hand.

The Boned Zone

The sucker puncher and the sucker clubber are sneak attackers and have probably already hit you or missed you through no skill of yours. Again, the instinct to move left after being hit from the left gets you out of his power arc and behind his weapon. Even among stick fighters that have trained for years most do not have a backhand that stops you. Blunt striking attacks tend to be forehand. If he has a backhand it sucks, and coming back after you with it is like giving you his arm or weapon.

If his backhand doesn't suck, congrats, you are either being mugged by a tennis pro or a world class stick fighter. Good luck.

The leftward step is a step and drag.

If you have a weapon in hand you slash or chop with it from right to left as you move from right to left, harnessing your motion for the stroke.

Having stepped left, if the situation calls for flight you stride forward with the right leg and run past him, not off to the side. Make him turn around to pursue.

If the situation calls for combat you now have both of your hands against his one hand, and go from there.

The Boned Zone

In all of your stick, knife and boxing training I suggest developing the MMA shield habit with the left hand. The right side of your head and face is the target for almost everything coming your way in hand to hand combat. If bringing that palm up to your temple is an ingrained habit, it could save your life and enhance this leftward stepping pass.

Get out of The Boned Zone ASAP.

Mister Al and the Thugess

The Genesis of The Boned Zone: the Conspiracy of the Liberal Elite and the Criminal Poor

Where does The Boned Zone, in its present form, originate? The Boned Zone was once the primal place where you ended your days in the jaws of a leopard or under a slathering pack of hyenas. What we have now is an evolved predatory matrix, where you have an immediate threat and then the overall threat supporting and justifying it. Let's use our distant ancestors as an example. For this sketch permit me to lean on a learned scholar's academically broad shoulders.

The Descent of Man, By T. Spoone Slickens, Inquire

Once upon a before hats were worn backwards and pants were worn below the butt time, Homobreakfast gets up in the morning from under the pile of hairy family members he sleeps with, picks up his sharpened femur bone, and goes down to the waterhole looking for breakfast. Once there his dimwitted ass finds out that he is breakfast for the thing that just clamped its jaws around his neck.

Ages of hairy misfortune continue. Eventually one particularly smart Homobreakfast uses his femur bone dagger to stab the leopard in the eye, killing it. He then uses his sharp rock shard to skin the leopard and becomes the leopard—an ass eating machine to reckon with! And God rewards him with the most fertile Homobreakfast honeydoll and, through her, he passes on his propensity for success, evolving eventually, by fits and starts, into us, Homoincorrectness.

Homoincorrectness wanders the asphalt and concrete savanna under a godless sky. You see, since the liberals killed God, they have set themselves up in his place. And where God once rewarded man with opportunity when he strove and survived, he is now punished.

Suppose Homoincorrectness has gotten up from sleeping underneath of his newspapers, and is wandering down to the waterhole to buy a pint of cheap vodka, whereupon he is attacked by Homoyowhazupus. Consider that Homoyowhazupus forget to bring his three friends and Homoincorrectness shoves this attacker out in front of a city bus. We might say, "good for that chump-ass thug."

Misfortunately the liberal Mamma God is now angry that one of her retarded chillens has been bested. She sends her blue angels, armed with thunder and lightning, don't you know, to haul Homoincorrectness off to purgatory or hell, depending on the whim of Liberal Heaven.

This would be like Homobreakfast killing that leopard that tried to eat him, only to have God yank a tree out of the ground and swat him like a fly.

And that is basically how Man went from master of all he surveys, to slave to that which rules according to the pollster's survey.

Mister Al and the Thugess

Mister Al is a Vietnam combat veteran who came home from the war and went to work for the CSX Railroad, where he retired as an inspector. Mister Al came to me looking for a post-retirement job as he claimed he was driving his dear wife crazy being at home all the time.

I didn't want to put an old man on merchandizing, as that's hard work. One slot I had a hard time filling with young men was parcel-pickup, which included light janitorial work, basically racking up carts, greeting customers, helping with bags, and sweeping the floor. Young guys would inevitably use this position to deal drugs. I hit on hiring men and paying them $10 an hour to not only show up on time and do the job, but call me to the front when they spotted criminals. This made a huge difference in making the store approachable for the elderly and decent.

Mister Al was perfect: polite, dressed in a suit and tie every day, showed up 10 minutes early, gave me a security and janitorial briefing before he left, and even wore his dress uniform on Memorial Day and the Fourth of July.

Unfortunately I got a lot of flak from the owners, Andy and his Dyke sister Mandy.

Andy, the CEO, only valued black men as dick-swinging Mandingo sex objects and cocaine suppliers. Therefore a decent black man was worthless. Andy also hated the elderly for some unexplained Freudian reason.

Mandy, the CFO, only valued menacing black men, continually asking me to hire "big intimidating black men" as a shield against criminals. She also disliked hiring older men, which she referred to as "the iron lung crew" citing the potential health insurance costs.

The Boned Zone

One day this well-dressed BMW driving ghetto bitch walked by Mister Al and dropped her fast food trash on the walk just after he swept it. He bent over to pick it up, shaking his head in disgust. Seeing him shake his head sent her into a fit of rage. She went off, calling him a "nigger" and "an Uncle Tom," and threatening to "beat" his "narrow ass." She spit on his dress slacks as well.

When she approached me about his rudeness I defended him and she threatened to have her lawyer husband "come up on me," which I suggested would be a great idea as he could obviously use a conversation with "someone who let him get a word in edgewise."

She walked off in a huff and contacted Andy and Mandy who wanted me to fire Mister Al to appease this bitch. I countered that we should give him a raise and bar her from the property as she was nasty to all of our employees, only purchased lottery tickets, and inconvenienced our full service customers.

We compromised by doing nothing and I gave Mister Al a $20 out of my pocket for his dry cleaning.

After I resigned Mister Al was among five other decent older people the owners got rid of. The front of the store is now an open drug market/panhandling zone, not safe for a lone woman to negotiate with her purse, just as it was before I showed up and ran the criminals off.

Andy and Mandy were the spoiled children of millionaires, who felt guilt and resentment in equal measure for their ill-earned affluence with every breath of their wretched souls.

The guilt for having it easy they attempted to divert by rewarding black criminals.

The resentment they felt for not being self sufficient they pushed down onto the heads of their struggling employees who were barely making ends meet, so that they could know the sadistic joy of seeing those who strive—as they had never had the necessity to—fail.

Andy was so sick with this sadism that he would beg me to let him fire deserving employees. When I denied him this outlet he would lash back at me by firing random employees on my day off. I once caught Andy masturbating in his office after firing a seafood clerk—who did deserve termination for theft, but not to be the object of Andy's orgasm.

The fact that this guy, who is a respected philanthropist and champion of the black community, would literally jack off in ecstasy at the thought of some poor—black or white—dude losing his $150 dollar per week job and getting evicted from a boarding house to sleep on the sidewalk, was enough to make me wretch.

Andy and Mandy are surely extreme prurient examples of the liberal white guilt sickness that infects the degenerate ruling class of postmodern society. But their actions—to punish the decent working poor and appease the criminal poor—these actions are as old as Caesar having bread thrown to the mob at the circus even as a million slaves toiled in chains to make that bread, and is, above all, a symbol of a society in decline. And just as a society on the incline emulates the upper class, a society on the decline emulates the lower class.

Want to See Some Real Riots?

A Hoodrat Apocalypse Countdown for the Surefire Urban Unrest Game Changer [With Blackout Update]

Blackout Update: As we come off a weekend that saw six bodies dropped in Harm City in 48 hours, and multiple children from age 8-13 shot, I walked past a house five blocks from my home where a 16 year old girl's body was pulled out by firemen, early Sunday morning. She was apparently killed in her grandmother's house before the fire was set and an autopsy has just been planned! I have definitely decided that I live in a new and nastier Baltimore than I did two months ago.

The buses—even the school bus I took home this morning—are still no more than 75% of normal capacity, which means many more people are using mass transit than two weeks ago. The interesting thing is the nature of the 25% mass transit user shortfall. The only people that have not resumed using the bus fall into two groups, the first tiny, the other large:

1. white women

2. the innocent unarmed black youth who normally cause problems for the driver, or who attack other youths, threaten adults, or otherwise make themselves a nuisance to law abiding people

I wonder what group 2 is doing. Perhaps they are no longer wannabe gangbangers but the real thing, recruited into the burgeoning drug war?

As I was mulling over these matters I received a call from Miss Ezz, Ghetto supermarket checkout manager, who had read this article.

"Hey Sugar, loved the EBT roadmap to urban oblivion. But you left something out. Whenever there is a power outage, a flood, or a bad storm, our customers get an immediate EBT distribution of two-hundred or four-hundred dollars, depending on how long the power was out. More free money! What if there is a power outage for a week, and these slackers don't get their one thousand dollars for their cable TV being cut off? Talk about a riot!"

"Also, with SSI, if the first of the month falls on a Saturday or a Sunday, the checks will come out on Friday.

"Stay safe, Baby Cakes!"

I stand corrected, me and all of me ghetto-babe pet name alter egos.

The Baltimore Riots and Purge could have been predicted based on the Fergusson affair, and, like Fergusson, will be repeated when the police trial verdicts come down. Local pharmacies have already begun boarding up their entire store fronts in anticipation of looting later this summer.

Taken in context the Baltimore riots were paltry next to the potential: a mere few hundred children battling the BPD to a standstill while a mere 200 business were looted out of thousands.

What do you think it would be like if the hoodrat adults joined the riots?

Imagine, instead of hundreds of young thugs, tens of thousands of all ages spilling down city streets like a ravenous flood of inequity!

What could—would—trigger this?

As recorded in *'Don' Dey Know People Gots Ta Eat!'* people who lived at the epicenter of the Baltimore Riots began threatening to loot the store where the police sub station is.

The one thing that will drive riots quicker than anything is a lapse—or God forbid—a halt, in welfare disbursements. For a worst case scenario make it the very last day of July, of any old year, and suppose that the U.S. government is bankrupt, or that the electronic transfer system is down from an EMP blast. What will the urban unrest trajectory be?

The Welfare Apocalypse

The following trajectory is based on government subsidy disbursement dates.

1st: SSI payments are not made, bringing hardship upon the elderly, the retarded, the handicapped, and the willfully disabled. There will be media flak and political appeasement, but no riots.

2nd: A third of welfare recipients do not get their EBT cash. Fortunately EBT cash is used primarily to buy lottery tickets, alcohol, cigarettes and drugs, and transfer money to loved ones under the care of the Federal Bureau of Prisons. Rather than looting we will likely see end of month levels of crimes such as shoplifting and strongarm robbery.

3rd: Two thirds of welfare recipients have not received their cash.

4th: All welfare recipients have not received their cash and the looting of liquor stores and newsstands begins in earnest.

5th: No free money comes out on the fifth, the hoodrats are used to this and should calm down to a simmer.

6th-15th: Beginning with the 6th, every day at midnight, hoodrats do not receive the food stamps that their last name's placement in the alphabet entitles them to. The pantries and refrigerators are empty. Since the government has so wisely put the poor on a once a month grocery shopping schedule, after 30 days of no significant shopping, the hoodrat larders are empty of scrimps, chicken wings, ramen noodles, pop tarts, soda pop, and juice boxes. This avalalnche of hunger, engineered by the federal government to do for the poor what the The Cool Spring Reservoir did for Uniontown, Pennsylvania in 1912, would, if EBT food stamp transfers were not received over this 10 day period, cause between 10,000 and 100,000 low income blacks to overrun Baltimore retailers.

That would be a riot.

'Girding Your Loins'

Notes on Media Paranoia and Domestic Sabotage from A Utility Worker

With the mess in Baltimore this past April our readership expanded significantly. The Jack Donovan review brought many masculinity readers. And Ann Sterzinger's Graphomaniac article brought a broader base of readers, as well as our first real influx of fiction readers since the beginning. The fact that one of the few people covering the Baltimore Riots without a media filter was this here crackpot brought at least five readers who seem to be involved in utility company operation and management, and a high influx of information technology experts. The email below comes from a person that works for a rural utility. Such people understand more about our social infrastructure than us urban apes have generally considered, as our social system is weighted towards ignorance of the masses. All the politician wants you to know about the power grid, is that when she says everything will be alright, that you believe her, and that some redneck in a utility truck will make it so.

[In reference to **Want To See Some Real Riots?**]

The Boned Zone

This is what I meant about girding your loins.

About 7 years ago we trained as a [deleted] company on emergency protocol. We rehearsed the earthquake. EMP, terrorism scenarios, but the one that got my attention was domestic sabotage. We were asked to come up with ideas on how to take down water systems. I think it scared the shit out of some people in administration. Your utility's are wide open, the problem is they are afraid of the operators too—we came up with some scary stuff. You never let educated rednecks time to think! They have seen both sides of the tracks, especially the military trained operators who now work in the utility companies.

We have first response badges we carry in case all hell breaks loose. We built these systems. Of course we know how to destroy them. But why would a sane human want to harm innocents, especially children? This is the problem with paranoia and the media, they work people, to sell, or watch their programs, but after reading some of your articles it makes me wonder too.

Best regards,

Samuel

Addendum

The utility companies: like power, natural gas, water, all know of the perils of sabotage. It makes my blood run cold, to think about it. But how can you cover all the bases of a vast network of interconnected systems. I don't know why we haven't been hit yet? The East Coast would be in deep trouble! Imagine no water or power, say for minimum of 2 weeks, any longer will bye-bye.

Maureen   June 7, 2015 3:44 PM EDT

Wow you write a lot. You write faster than I can read it. Have a nice day!

 **responds:** June 8, 2015 4:52 PM EDT

I had some help with this one.

Have a nice sunny day out their on the Left Coast.

Martha and the Media Torch

Sam Dickson: "A Benediction for Heretics"

Thanks to VDare for the heads up had through the link below sent by a supporter:

"We all have the soft spot for the polish catholic grit. Reminds me of how you could not wrap your head around the attention given to dead thugs but none to a woman and baby murdered in the same time frame."

http://www.vdare.com/articles/unequal-justice-martha-stewart-jailed-for-lying-to-police-but-ferguson-witnesses-not-prosecuted

I am reminded, on hearing this speech, that the ancient Hellenes regarded the spoken word to be truer than the written, the script version being merely a ghostly echo of the true spirit of inquiry. Not surprisingly this YouTube feed seems to be a might sluggish, as if it is being broadcast from the muffled back of the recently reorganized societal bus.

I would remind the race realists that, when dealing with the media, we are dealing with a fantastical dimension infused with less truth than your grandson's cartoon video game. The criminal who lied to the cops, and made up the entire Tiny Teen Fergusson martyr legend from whole cloth to save his own hide, was a bonanza to the media; the veritable torch that lit the ratings flame that is now the unquenchable fire of urban-unrest race-baiting journalism. The media is perched like a vulture from hell, positioned to ride the updraft into the long American night.

https://www.youtube.com/watch?v=AqGD1NLkQO8

'I Know a Bitch When I Deal With Him'

Harm City Bus Altercation: 19 Line, 5:43 p.m., 7/7/15

After a good deal of training I was boarding the #19 bus out in Towson, heading back into what Solomon Kane would have called The Pit, but which I call home. The Africa woman who had been speaking to me was let onboard first by all of the men, 2 Mexicans, 1 big white guy in a dress shirt and tie, and two black dudes. The big white dude was a real traditionalist, at only 35 years, even insisting that my old ass gets on before him.

Five minutes later, just inside the City line in the mini ghetto of the Dutch Village apartments, two muscular black men boarded, one large and arguing on his phone with a domineering woman, the other small, coal black, not possessed of a bus ticket, and impatient with the driver's insistence that he pay. At about 50 years of age he was ignoring the driver, pretending to count out a potential bus fare.

This is the scheduling gambit, where it is known that a driver at the head of a line is loath to get behind on his schedule arguing a point of payment. I can tell by his body language that the apish little man has no intention of paying, as he recounts the same three coins over and over again, his back to the driver, who does move off. The idea behind the scheduling gambit is to get a ride for a few blocks, then discover that you did not have enough change, and ask to be put off.

The big white guy sitting forward of me noticed the man ignoring the driver, and seeking to keep society running smoothly by reminding him that the bus driver has addressed him, said something with a polite tone that was not loud enough to be audible to me, three seats back.

Oh, know he didn't!

I was laughing before the altercation had reached middle age.

"Who you talkin' to?"

As soon as the white man tried to explain that there was no malice intended he was lost, drawn into a bitch-making pimp trap as the perspective bitch.

"Oh, I sure as hell know you ain't talkin' ta me, bitch!"

The Boned Zone

The bus driver yelled back, "Whoa, whoa, hold up!"

The little negmudgeon, noting the heft and weight of the voice of the Mandingo driver, as well as his looming bulk, glanced at the progress the bus had made, noted that he was now at the Pakistani Gas Station of Infinite Delights, that was his destination in any case, and said, "I don't got the fare, I'll get off here."

The white guy, finally in argument mode as the nasty little ghettoite reached the door and the driver sighed relief, said, "That's right, get off, bitch."

The driver groaned.

I put away my book; Andy Nowicki set aside for Flave-O-Flave minus his gold clock.

The little man walked up to the white man and said, "Say it again?"

The white man declined silently.

"Say it again, bitch—say it!"

The man declined silently.

"That's right—who da bitch now! Not only is you a bitch, but yo mutha a bitch, and yo granmutha a dick-suckin' bitch—swalloin' the pipe back in the good ole day!"

The man sat silently, just pointing to the door held open by the driver, indicating that the righteous little man should step off.

"Step off with me, bitch. Come on, step off."

The man silently declined.

"Oh, I knew I was dealin' with a bitch. I know a bitch when I deal with him. You won' swing fo yo mutha, won' even throw down ova yo dick-suckin' granny! You a bitch, a naked, raw, lickin' my balls, bitch! See, a real nigger would have swung, would have throwed down."

He walked to the front door and then turned wrathfully, having had a far more significant free ride than he could have imagined; emerging as a prince from a conveyance he had boarded as a measly pauper. "You know what, you disgust me. I won' ride a bus with the likes of your sorry bitch ass—and yo mamma too!"

Off our hero strutted into the slanting rays of the descending sun.

The Boned Zone

Never argue with blacks, or negrofied whites, in an African American Ethical Zone. There is literally nothing good that can come of it.

Jeremy Bentham   June 8, 2015 9:06 PM EDT

Good point James about never verbally engaging. No sort of "verbal judo" is likely to be very effective in those situations, since in most cases the hood-rats will have already made the decision to kick your ass. What do they have to fear? Nothing you can say then, no clever remark you can come up with, will be likely to dissuade them from their violent course of action. In fact, any reply you make to their taunts or other ploys to gain your attention will likely have the opposite effect, like a trigger word. Like Sergeant Greg Parker on "Flashpoint" saying "Scorpio". Further, given the current political climate, your words are even likely to provide the hood-rats with a readymade excuse for their actions, should they even have to explain themselves. Best to keep moving, to not respond to anything said to you and get out of the "kill zone" / "boned zone" as quickly as possible!

Actually I do not live in Suburbia James. I live in the outer belt of small cities circling a large metropolitan area. After roughly an hour's drive though, I can be in the center of a city just as messed up and crime ridden as Baltimore. A city that has descended into chaos for the identical reasons that Harm City has. The crazy thing, the supreme irony, is that in the peaceful little town I currently live in I am allowed by law to go out in public armed to the teeth, with guns, knives, clubs, pepper spray and stun guns (the state now has a very permissive "shall Issue" concealed carry license system). Whereas you dear James, who dwells in the heart of darkness, must rely on a mere bumbershoot for your defense. There is some small hope that the very worst societal decay might be limited to the major cities, since in my state the Woman has suffered severe defeats politically. The people have in recent years pushed back hard against the chaos and PC lunacy The Woman has inflicted on them. But the fight is far from over; The Woman remains strong and insolent. She is filled with fury at having been thwarted and her minions work tirelessly to destroy all those who would oppose her will. We'll keep praying for you James. May the Lord fill you with strength for battle and guide the strike of your bumbershoot.

Jeremy Bentham   June 8, 2015 1:27 PM EDT

"Democracy is the theory that the common people know what they want and deserve to get it good and hard."— H.L. Mencken

Yes James, it is at once sad and comical, is it not? The white people in Harm City long ago handed control of their city over to the Leftists, who promptly handed control over to the blacks. Clearly the Left was not completely honest and forth coming about what they wanted to accomplish when they asked for the votes of the working class white Harm City dwellers years ago (Surprise!). Note that journalist H.L. Menken was at one time called the "Sage of Baltimore". Did he understand something in particular about the future trajectory of local politics? Nevertheless, many of the said same white folks still haven't figured out it's the black people who are now firmly in control of events and can say and do whatever they want. Including delaying a city bus merely because they don't have the money to pay the fare. Plus The Woman expects white people to be the "adult" in any interaction with one of her oppressed non-white children. Therefore, it is incumbent upon the white person not to initiate any altercation with an individual belonging to an officially recognized a non-white oppressed group, regardless of the provocation. Rather the white person should suffer in silence whenever an oppressed man/woman child insists on being difficult. Certainly whites should refrain from hurling gratuitous insults. Just as it would be unseemly to the public at large for an adult to trade insults and threats with child, so also will the Woman frown upon whites engaging in pissing contests with her oppressed chilluns. Plus, as you have pointed out numerous times James, verbal arguments in the ghetto can quickly escalate into physical combat (faster than you might imagine possible). Are you prepared to deal with the possible consequences of this? If not, best to refrain from any comment. So white folks, be "situationally aware" at all times of where you are and what can happen there.

responds: June 8, 2015 5:02 PM EDT

I would have to say that the number one most important, most required, and most productive survival strategy in majority black urban environments is absolutely not to engage verbally with the criminal class.

The Boned Zone

Menken really got the character of urban Baltimore. I think what he was predicting was that the influx of rural blacks from the south, with better work habits and more gentile manners than the rude native Baltimoreans of both races, were going to be blunted, corrupted, and turned into what they have become, a reflection of the lesser angels of our nature, as fostered by the Liberal Left, which has controlled this city for over three generations.

BTW, our mayor has just cut police patrols in half as she waits for the hopeful fulfillment of her request for 20 million dollars in FEMA relief to rebuild what she instructed the police to let burn!

Enjoy suburbia Jeremy. Hopefully The Left will never do to suburbia what they've done to the cities.

'Asking For It'

Man From Brooklyn Tries To Start A Fight On The Subway But Ends Up Getting Got

[Based on a couple of comments by readers, one of which is at the bottom, I think I was wrong to call the whites in this film 'Pathetic', but will retain the original text. The smaller white person appears, on closer inspection, to be a female, and that changes everything.]

Welcome to the African American Ethical Zone when it comes down on Whitey's side. Keep in mind that every day, in every majority black American urban enclave, that many black men are beaten down by groups of black men in service to their ever devolving simian ethos. They are more likely to target blacks than whites as that is totally off the police radar. The important thing to note, is this is how this guy has been treated by other black men with which he is not bonded, and is likely a cause for his generic unfocused aggression against smaller, weaker non-cohesive whites—who come off as pathetic on this video.

The most important thing a lone white can do is stand up to him and make certain not to attract the ire of the predatory group hovering around, by, for instance, not using the one word that the group uses to describe him. Those guys are dangerous even when just having fun. When the lead thug tells the fool that if he starts it up against, "it's over" that means he will be stomped into a coma.

https://www.youtube.com/watch?v=S1hWSvpcg7o

MF   June 14, 2015 2:03 AM EDT

Maybe pathetic is a bit strong but there is a weakness seen here, this guy was willing to use his body as a shield for his girl but was still passive in his defense. A caribbean latino would have responded quite differently to this with his female and in a superior fashion to the white. I would not be surprised if the said female friend secretly was ashamed of her 'protector' deep down inside..another reason to reject female companionship!

The three goons were egging it on and darwin award winner turned his supporters into his enemies. Justice can come from the strangest places.

Subway cars are moving underground tomb/coffins where you are trapped with the living (brain) dead..and their necromancers

live high above in crystal spires. Goddamned Gotham.

responds: June 14, 2015 6:52 AM EDT

Honestly weak is a far more appropriate term than pathetic. I want to retain the pathetic remark from the original post because that came from the gut, and demonstrates that I am not always the calculating creature a writer has a tendency to make himself out to be.

Yes, friend, let us remain beyond the grip of the necromancers—women, so I hear...

jr   June 13, 2015 2:23 PM EDT

James, why did you think the whites looked so pathetic? Bearded man was obviously protecting his friend (cohesion!), who looked very young, and he did it effectively. The other white/hispanic just minded his own business, something you counsel.

responds: June 14, 2015 12:07 AM EDT

You are right J.R. I thought the little twerp was a guy, but a friend who sent me the link said it was a woman, in which case, the bearded guy did okay. I am a sexist. If the small timid person were a dude, as I originally thought, I would still be critical of him. But he is a her, and she gets a pass. More aggressive defenses by the bearded mate might have brought in the other blacks on the side of the guy they ended up beating.

Jimbob: The Interview

A Monologue on Stoner Culture by the Man Who Inspired Planet Buzzkill's Hero Stoner Joe

Last Tuesday morning I ran into my former roommate, Jimbob, while boarding the cross town bus. I was headed home from East Baltimore County and him to work from East Baltimore. Still lean of frame, he has worked in restaurants for most of his sixty odd years, but has also been a carney and a water tank jockey, tasked with insulting men into throwing baseballs at the target that would dump him into the water tank from his opinionated perch.

How big of a pothead was Jimbob?

When Jimbob and I both lived at the old plantation house he would get off work at 4, have a few drinks at the bar, bring home some beer, and by 5 be settled into his basement man cave hitting the bong. He would smoke pot from 5 p.m. Friday until 10 p.m. Sunday! By Sunday afternoon I would leave the house from my room two stories up so that I would not absorb any THC and test positive on a random drug test at work. Jimbob used to stand on the sidewalk two feet from the street on weekday evenings [the landlord did not tolerate pot smoking on weekday evenings] and smoke a joint while reading a book—and he is a well read man.

Once I saw him waving to a cop that was driving by. After I complimented him on his stoner elan he said, in his deep, cavernous voice with that raspy smoker's edge, "It works fine until you pass a joint to one of the fuckers. Then they either take it—if you're lucky—or lock you up."

As we sat down next to each other on the bus I asked him how he was doing.

"Doing good, man, working as a chef at the *&%@# Tavern. I take the bus in, the wife picks me up from work. Got married—finally abandoned the He-man Woman Haters Club, for a woman who pays my rent and buys my reefer. Can't beat that. I'm a kept man brother, not bad after a life alone.

"What about you, you still writing?"

"Yes, in fact one of my most-liked books is Planet Buzzkill, in which an unlikely pot-smoking hero, based on you, discovers that the alien invaders are allergic to THC."

Jimbob was off and running:

"Your choice of drug includes the consideration of a number of factors—one of them, of course, being the possibility of alien invasion—which, in the end, comes down to what kind of people you want to live with. Sol, for instance, is a crack head, just got locked up for fighting again. Crack is a violence drug. Do I want to live with violence? No.

"Do I want to live in a crack house paying rent to a guy like Sol who will eventually threaten or attack me, and then when I go after him with a machete I'm all of a sudden the bad guy? No.

"Of course, when I was coming up in the seventies there was no such thing as crack. It didn't exist.

"Cocaine was expensive—and still is—and the people that do it tend to be rich or snobbish despite of being poor and not good people to be around.

"Beer and wine is something that most people handle without getting violent. But you have to pick your friends carefully if you are a drinker because you have the psychotic cross-over crack heads, and the fact that one-in-five drunks are angry drunks. So if you're drinking keep it close and keep it small: small bar, drinking at home with close friends, etcetera.

"Heroin—yeah right. Have you ever seen anyone on heroin? That does not look like anyone's idea of a good time and is the only thing I haven't tried. It's a suicide drug. Fuck that. A three-fifty-seven to the temple is cheaper *and* quicker.

"LSD—acid—can be a good time if you like watching the world melt and you get a kick out of being paranoid. But if you're OCD or have a persecution complex—Jesus Christ, don't drop any acid! Acid is a good eight hour high if you are into thinking you're being attacked by speeding demons while you're driving down the interstate at ten miles per hour afraid that the state cops are coming for you. But the after effect is a two day headache. No thanks. That got old, and quickly.

"Pills—the idea of pills, of giving into the Medical Industrial Complex—never appealed to me, don't know a thing about them.

"Whiskey is bad news, guaranteed violence. Whiskey drinkers either brood—not a lot of fun there, what did your dog die of again?—or violent; too much of the wrong kind of fun. I mean it's what the blacks drink and they can't stay out of prison, so stay away from it.

The Boned Zone

"Now pot, if you like to relax with a good book, and you're not driven to write one, is a great high. The only two things that you do better on pot is eat and sleep. Everything else will be subpar, and you can forget the short term memory—which is no big loss if you don't experience anything in your day to day life that is worth remembering, and can be a big plus if you live with some asshole that tells the same joke every day."

Jimbob' stop was coming up, and as he stood, the handful of delinquent high school kids that surrounded us on the bus, all looked up to him like members of a cargo cult mournfully watching the aviator whose mode of flight they worshipped rise far above and out of reach.

'The Deeper Savagery of the Pack'

Let Us Salute the Flag: ON THE NOBILITY OF MOTIVES By Fred Reed, June 15, 2015

Lately I've been missing Fred Reed's posts as I've been caught up on reporting the increased crime in my particular war zone. But thanks to Ishmael I was treated to this update on Fred's [he is an ex-Marine Vietnam Veteran] anti-war literature. In this article Fred makes a case for our current brand of patriotism being an 'after-market add-on' and that our military men are not engaged in anything particularly noble.

I only have one thing to add to his piece, that the men who go into the military, and then return home, will eventually form the leadership for the various factions in the coming American Civil War, just as the Mexican War Veterans did for the North and the South 12 years after. Street gangs send men into the military to get there training for a reason. This will be a fractional civil war with many a regional front and that which is learned murdering enemies, and innocents, overseas will eventually be employed here in what will figure to be turmoil of karmic proportions.

For me the wild card is the U.S. military. Will the active military actually participate in the coming unrest, or will it be left to contractors, like the goons that stopped me when the curfew came down seven weeks ago? Ever since then, every time I speak with the man I was with when the four unidentified operatives rolled up on an American illegally walking on his home town's street two blocks from his house with a friend, one of us has just said out of the blue, "Who were those guys?"

I'm wondering if other Americans across the country are soon going to have such, "Who were those guys?" moments? I am hoping, but not trusting, that the majority of military veterans will weigh in on the human side and not work as government contractors.

Check out Fred's view of the current military at the link below.

https://www.lewrockwell.com/2015/06/fred-reed/dont-honor-the-troops/

B June 21, 2015 6:21 AM EDT

Hennisart's book is, in my opinion, great because it deals not with the war but with the politics of what happened once the French military won the war, at great political expense and by exposing themselves to total vilification by the better classes of French society (and they had to murder lots of people back in the Metropole, too-they had dozens of bound Arabs washing up on the banks of the Seine: https://en.wikipedia.org/wiki/Paris_massacre_of_1961).

DeGaulle used the victory to consolidate power over his political scene, then promptly sold Algiers, which had been a part of France in all respects, out to the FLN, betraying not only the hundreds of thousands of soldiers who'd suffered there, but also the Pieds Noirs, the ethnic French who'd been living there for over a century, the hundreds of thousands of Algerian Harkis who'd fought for the French, and the millions of Arabs who just wanted to live their lives, make a living, have kids and so on, for whom the France had assumed responsibility when they conquered the place. Of course, this was done to please the Americans, who'd put huge pressure on France and other European colonial powers over the prior decade and a half.

A minority of the French military and right wing took offense to this hideous betrayal, conspired and fought. As Hennisart describes, the O's immediately folded like laundry. Some of the true believers fought an underground war of terror in Algiers and the Metropole for years before being captured, tried and executed.

The other indispensable book on Algiers is Aussaresses' tell-all, where octogenarian Uncle Aussaresses, a terrifying 20th century badass, casually describes how, after transitioning from scholar to WW2 hero and post-WW2 commando officer with the occasional civilian intelligence detail, he was sent to Algiers, where immediately encountered a massacre of French civilians by the Arabs they'd been living and working with. Then he had it explained to him what his function would be: since the political fiction that Algiers was a part of France, with rule of law, courts, law enforcement and the rest, was indispensable, and since in a guerrilla war, courts, law enforcement and the penal are completely unequipped to handle the numbers and gravity of the crimes being committed, someone would need to fill the gap. That would be him, leading a task force of guys who would find the enemy leadership, kidnap them, torture them and execute them, unofficially, of course. Just like by peacetime standards, a guerrilla platoon commits, in a week, enough crimes for a mid-sized city for a year, Aussaresses and his guys were completely hideous criminals by those same standards. He recounts all this in detail, with wonderful black Gallic humor.

America doesn't really have a Trajan's Column for its foreign conquests. By the time it got around to being an empire, it had been captured by Unitarian cuckold-theology that saw conquest and rule as shameful. Not to be celebrated. The closest thing is post-Civil War architecture in the big East Coast cities-Union Hall in NYC and all that.

Special ops guys are like the rest of the military, but more so. There are cosmetic differences that allow you to keep, on a daily basis, more humanity, individuality and warrior honor, but it's not by an order of magnitude. No hope from that quarter-I don't think in 6 years I met anyone of Aussaresses' caliber.

My search is done. I'm a Jew, I live in my land, on a hilltop in Samaria. I make kids, worship G-d and build as

I can. We're about the biggest source of irritation to the New York Times out there, as a country and a community. If they're agin' it, I'm for it.

JL **responds:** June 21, 2015 7:56 AM EDT

> Thanks so much for the links and the history brief, B. The books on the Legion Estranger tend to gloss over the Algerian question. I will seek out these titles.

> Using the New York Times editorial bias as a benchmark for evil, is, I think, as clear an ethos as running water.

B June 16, 2015 8:48 PM EDT

During the last several years of my military time, I was hoping for a coup.

Then I read Hennisart's Wolves In The City.

The French generals were a lot tougher and better educated than almost anyone in US uniform today. They'd started off doing Jedburgh team jumps into occupied France in WW2, went on through the meat grinder of Indonesia (many through Dien Bien Phu) and Algeria. In the meantime, they'd gotten real educations, not degrees in Business Management from West Dickhole State like your typical US officer.

Yet when they tried to launch a coup against their govt, which was obviously betraying their country, they failed miserably, turning on each other and crawling to De

Gaulle for forgiveness within days.

I understood that a career spent in a careerist organization has the effect of undermining character and training/selecting for poor moral courage, and that nobody in the US military with the rank and position to plan and launch a coup had the courage to do so successfully. I started looking for a new social value system.

Perhaps the guys coming back will run various factions in the American Civil War, but I suspect most of them will come down on the side of whatever looks most like the State.

As for Fred-he's a bit hypocritical, since his whole shtick throughout his writing career has been built on his combat service in Vietnam. That said, American public pro-military sentiment is largely of the Walmart/UFC kind. Hard to get really excited about the latest War in Dacia, but good form to thank the legionnaires.

 **responds:** June 19, 2015 7:38 AM EDT

B,

Thanks so much for this post.

I did read four books on the French Foreign Legion, which I was fascinated with from childhood. I recall one of the authors interviewing a U.S. Marine sergeant at joint maneuvers off of Corsica, who expressed admiration for the Legion. I find your Dacian comment interesting, evoking as it does an older legion—but an imperial tool nonetheless.

What is our Trajan's column, in your opinion?

Are our special ops people—as warriors coming from a feminized non-warrior society—essentially like a foreign legion?

I hope your search is going well, sir.

Jeremy Bentham   June 15, 2015 11:02 PM EDT

"Pacifism is objectively pro-fascist. This is elementary common sense. If you hamper the war effort of one side, you automatically help out that of the other. Nor is there any real way of remaining outside such a war as the present one. In practice, 'he that is not with me is against me'." – George Orwell

"The quickest way of ending a war is to lose it." – George Orwell

'The Troll Cop'

Kim's Insane Traffic Stop

Kim and her mother [a middle aged woman] were headed down to the Eastern Shore of the Chesapeake Bay across the Bay Bridge. They were working for WIC as undercover agents, attempting to buy the wrong items in food stores authorized to accept Department of Agriculture WIC [Women Infants Children] vouchers. The Department of Agriculture, unlike other agencies that subsidize food purchases, takes fraud seriously.

"I was pulled over for doing seventy-four in a fifty five zone by a bridge cop, a troll who only works the bridge. He asked me if I had been drinking and I told him that I had had a margarita for lunch. He insisted on giving me a breathalyzer, which I was okay with. But my mother started yelling at him that we were working under cover for WIC and then got out of the truck. He told her to get back in the truck and she did. Then she got out the other side and told him to go fuck himself. So he threw her on the ground and cuffed her.

"I was looking at my mom handcuffed in the police cruiser and was really nervous. This troll cop was a real dick, and he was also out of control. He gave me the breathalyzer over and over and over again as he yelled at me. He kept saying that I was ruining the test. Finally, he told me to blow harder—that he was giving me one last chance—and, thank God, it worked and I was not under the influence.

"Finally some real cops pulled up and they couldn't believe how he was acting. They told me that he had been a narcotics cop in the city and that something went down that was not right and he was assigned to the bridge as a punishment. He didn't want to be a troll cop on the bridge so he was looking for a big arrest. I felt so much better with the real cops there.

"Then he searches the truck, which I had just inherited from my father, who had just passed away, and had not cleaned out yet. He pulls out this big machete that my father had spray-painted fluorescent yellow for some reason, and began waving it around and said, "Ah ha!"

"He also found my two cartons of cigarettes which I had bought in West Virginia. Everybody thinks you are allowed two cartons of out of state cigarettes, but, in Maryland, its two packs! They gave me two packs and took the rest—I suppose smoked them. I was arrested for concealing a deadly weapon and for transporting cigarettes with the intent to distribute.

"I wanted a jury trial, which really freaked them out. So they offered me this plea; they would drop everything—no points for speeding, which I really wanted—and only charge me with two year's supervised probation for the machete. I wrote a letter to the court and got them to reduce it to one year and they had to return my father's machete. So I get arrested for having a machete in the truck that I did not know was in the truck, but am allowed to walk out of a courtroom and down the street with the thing under my arm?

"I saw the probation officer three times. Mind, you, I am a grown woman. The only thing that the probation officer was worried about—she was a woman—was whether or not I had any contact with my mother! Of course I'm not going to stay away from my mother because the court doesn't want me to see her. Besides, we worked together! What a joke."

"After that the kids started calling me Madam Machete."

Be mindful that The Boned Zone is not only stalked by hoodrats and thugs, but by pigs, the deadliest enemy a U.S. citizen can confront. They are God with a Gun and they know it. So by all means do not tell your friendly neighborhood pig to go fuck himself.

Last week, when I was at the local bar with Mescaline Franklin and Quinn, in a neighborhood where pigs drive right by packs of hoodrats hanging round the ATM machine, where Big Jim, the White Vice Lords and I are the only white pedestrians who have not been mugged, and where businesses are already boarding up for the next round of black youth riots, a white thirty something pig, walked into the bar and stared us all in the eyes one by one, in a limp-wristed attempt to intimidate men who were mostly 20 years older than him and had no criminal records, but worked, unlike his parasitic ass.

That is, what we call in Harm City, "a police" and "that's how they do."

The policeman is not your friend, but you must be his or you will pay. Call the asshole in the phony military outfit, "sir," until he's done flexing his blueceps.

B June 16, 2015 3:55 PM EDT

Hi, Jim,

I don't call the cops "sir." I talk to them in a quiet, relaxed, conversational manner, like they are my buddy,

The Boned Zone

without showing stress or fear, without volunteering information beyond that what is asked and without being evasive.

It's like dealing with a strange, dangerous dog. The dog doesn't know what to make of you initially, and if you don't register as a threat or prey, will move onto something else pretty quickly.

To Neglect and Disturb

Notes from the Post-Purge Pork Beat

The Evil Oracle

This past Friday night there was a 'police involved shooting' at the #19 bus stop at the corner of Harford and Hamilton Avenue. The media has reported that an MTA police officer—who one might suspect of having a chip on his shoulder since his small force got steamrolled in the late April Hoodrat offensive—shot a person of unknown race, age or gender in the leg. The withholding of information about the 'suspect' in such an encounter is usually code for unarmed, innocent, black teenager.

Speaking with witnesses who were actually watching the encounter, this non-journalist has found that the altercation was quite different then that reported by the media. The MTA cop noticed a youth packing a gun and commanded them to comply with a search, at which point the youth ran, and was grappled by the cop. During the course of the altercation the youth shot himself in the leg.

I can understand withholding the observation that the shooting of oneself in the leg with a gun which one is declining to give to his attacker, might reasonably indicate an attempt to shoot one's attacker. As logical as this is, it is just conjecture, and I would not expect to see it in news coverage, even in a pro law-enforcement publication. However, to infer in print and broadcast media that this cop was shooting at a fleeing youth is a gross misrepresentation that is obviously calibrated to incite more unrest among the feral natives of Harm City. I read this as another indication that our liberal ruling elite and their media priesthood are dedicated to fomenting civil unrest. Since, in all of my years as a mass transit user, I have never seen a white MTA cop, I am hoping this officer is of the usual color. Police in Baltimore finally began asserting themselves over the youth thugs again this time last week. It would be a shame to have the media roll that back so soon, what with another Freddie Gray purge in our future.

The Babe Behind the Scenes

Elisa works for the Baltimore City Police Department. Although I have promised to keep her job description confidential, she does do work associated with maintaining the BPD Motor Pool. According to her the damage to police vehicles and the numbers of police vehicles lost in the late April riots, was grossly underreported, and the vehicle maintenance and acquisition process is still a huge unresolved headache.

This is just another small example of the propaganda spin that has misinformed every level of the Baltimore Riot/Purge coverage. I expect, for the next round of riots, that media coverage will be more opaque and government-friendly in its obfuscation of the facts on the ground than it was for the first round of riots.

Fried Chicken to Go

Jenny works at a convenience store in Baltimore County. It is of extreme interest to me that during the week of the riots Baltimore County Police abandoned most of their duties to focus on securing the County Seat. What is even more interesting is the fact that nighttime police coverage in the Essex Precinct [which was the most violent County precinct in 2013, and became the most improved precinct in 2014] is still around 25% of what it was prior to the riots, and that daylight coverage is slightly less than the previous normal.

Where have these cops gone?

Police no longer look in on Abner at the 7-11 after dark.

We rarely see them at the supermarket anymore, even as the panhandlers and dope fiends become more threatening to staff and customers.

I asked Jenny about this. Stuck behind the convenience store counter in a lonely spot from 11 p.m. to 6 a.m., she had felt safe up until two weeks ago. The shift manger was the wife of a police officer, and authorized free fried chicken meals for police officers.

"The cops always said that they didn't just stop in for the chicken, but were concerned about our safety. Well, since that manger quit her job and we haven't had a replacement manager to authorize the free police meals, we have not seen a single cop—not one in two weeks! How long before the crooks figure this out and come for me—put a gun in my face?"

Enclave Policing?

These are a few small glimpses of a new Baltimore Area police paradigm that in few ways resembles the one previous to the riots. I am fascinated that the County Police have so changed their habits in the wake of an unrest event that was largely confined to the city.

The Boned Zone

Although there was a purge of lone white males by packs of black males in the county precinct I am discussing, it occurred in part because there was **zero** police coverage in that precinct while the riots and purge were ongoing in the city. I understand pulling all officers out of working class precincts to staff upper class areas during a crisis. After all, policing is at root the management of the lower classes for the benefit of the upper class. But I do not understand why normal policing has not resumed in outlying areas.

The MTA shooting occurred at the center of a hipster/yuppie enclave, a viable example of urban gentrification, five feet from one of the three businesses owned by the leader of the community association. 16 hours after the shooting, I walked by the spot, checked for blood stains and found disappointingly little, and headed over to the Hamilton bakery to meet Terry and friends for her wedding cake tasting. [I never knew there was such a thing.] This upscale bakery is run by a left coast couple who seemed leery of me when I walked in in sleeveless shirt and shorts. The man told me he heard the single shot. He was also cheered by the two police cars bracketing the two block business district with lights on, behaving like mall cops.

A hipster couple and their infant then walked in off the street from the fine dining and drinking establishment next door. I knew this because he was carrying an open beer bottle and drinking from it. He was enjoying a Fat Tire IPA. That is okay with me. Hell, I don't even believe in laws, let alone some law as nannyish as an open container law. However, I reminded Terry, if that had been White Howard, Quinn, Russ, me or Mescaline stepping out of the sports bar and walking down the sidewalk drinking a National Boh, we would have been stopped by one of those cops and either arrested or given a citation.

My inner self is cheered by the fact that this node, of this evil materialistic society I have lived in contention with my entire slave's life, has fractured apart so easily and so unconsciously based on a mere week of domestic unrest by less than 1% of the population! Perhaps the door of the decrepit America House is more rotten than I had supposed. Perhaps I'll live long enough to see it kicked in, or simply fall from the weight of its own rotten gain.

The Survival Stick

A Combat Question from Mira

"James, I am a woman who lives alone and am interested in an effective and practical hand weapon, such as the fighting stick you described in your article *'Making My Own Fighting Stick'*. There is a man on the west coast that has a studio and makes sticks, who I Googled. He said that a pair of sticks would cost $15 plus shipping and handling. Is there anything else I should know about defending with the stick, and are there any additional material dimensions I should be aware of?"

Thank you, Mira

Dimensions

That price is reasonable, Mira.

As for sticks, keep in mind that they are primarily training tools and legal alternatives to the man-stopping

tools we really need to keep the savage world at bay—
so upgrade when possible.

Mira, as with any implement used by a woman, there is
a perfect length and girth for a blunt extension weapon,
relative to her hand size and arm length.

The girth of the weapon should permit you to touch
either your ring or middle finger to the muscle at the
base of the thumb. The minimal girth would permit you
to fully encircle the weapon while the hand is still
relaxed and you have not engaged the flexor muscle and
tendon on the outside of the forearm to pull the butt of
the stick closer to the wrist. The maximum girth would
give separation from the closing fingers and thumb side
of the palm when relaxed but contact when flexed.

A handy weapon for use indoors should not exceed the
length of a cubit, or that from your elbow to the tip of
your extended fingers.

A compact weapon for use inside a car or in a clinch or
access way, should not exceed the length of the forearm
bones from elbow to wrist.

A walking weapon, for use on your feet in the
outdoors, should not exceed the length of your arm and

hand as measured from the armpit to the inside of the last digit of the longest finger.

Man Note: For a male combat athlete trained with the stick, the weapon length is practical so long as it does not exceed the length of his arm as measured from the outside of the shoulder socket to the tip of the middle finger.

Materials

As a woman, we are not too concerned with your legal liability [unless you are dealing with a female or helpless unarmed innocent black youth] and are primarily concerned with you having the most effective weapon legally tenable for the setting. With women home invasions are a huge concern. There should be a weapon within reach from your front porch to your safe room, in every living space and access way of the house. In case you have been burgled in the day light and the intruder has had a chance to pick up a weapon you have left in reach for yourself, you want to make sure that the materials of the weapons that lie deepest in your home are superior to those on the periphery; a stick by the door and a sword next to your bed.

The Boned Zone

When out and about, a rattan or hardwood walking stick for protection against dogs of the four-legged, two-legged and most of all, three-legged varieties, will suffice.

In your car, it's the last day on earth, Girl. The police will burn you for having a blade in the car, so go with a compact rod of solid steel or iron, a hardened flashlight, a tire iron, or a short-handled ball peen hammer.

On your front porch keep a potted plant at the base of your door, with a handy white oak stick disguised as a planting stake.

Just inside the door you want a compact steel pipe.

In your kitchen you have an arsenal. Go with the butcher knife.

In the bathroom keep a scuba knife, flashlight, titanium curling iron, a geisha assassin hair pin, or compact stainless steel bar.

In your safe room, or bed room, you want a weapon at the door such as a bowie knife, at the dresser or desk such as a combat infantryman's knife, and under your pillow an assassin's dagger. If you are called upon to leave your safe room to aid a family member against an intruder you should be able to emerge with a blade in each hand. When the goon grabs you saw his guts out with the other hand and poke holes in him until he stops squirting.

As a man, my arsenal is heavier in my room. In my bed is a bowie knife, on the night stand a dagger, by the dresser a late medieval arming sword, at my desk a pair of butterfly swords, by my foot locker a Viking sword and a jobolo wood baton, and by the door to my room a hickory walking stick, a razor sharp daito [ninja sword] and a 14 inch meat hook. I want to emerge from my room with a weapon in each hand, as such a scenario would be triggered by an audible break in or an attack on my housemates—and, for that apocalyptic event, I have my bow and arrows.

The weapons in your room should be a mix of edged handy and compact edged for defense against surprise intrusions, at least one full length blade for a possibly sally against an intruder, as well as a full length blunt weapon, like a crow bar, for sallying into the yard to perhaps rescue a dog who is being abducted for pitbull bait, a child being eaten by the neighbor dog, your crazy mother who picked a fight with your Salvadoran landscaper, or your sissy boy toy who is getting mugged by a pack of twelve year old ghetto girls...

Keep all three lengths of weapon in their appropriate zones, with an assortment available in your safe room to cover different contingencies. Above all, Mira, keep in mind that you live in a predatory matrix, and that she without claws or fangs is halfway to becoming a meal.

When they come for you in the public, predatory friendly, spaces patrolled by our masters, who wish us to be defenseless, smash their hands, break their jaws and bash in their heads. When they come for you in your home, rip them open and run them through.

When your back is to the wall, make war on the world— it deserves no less.

Mark Lawrence   June 26, 2015 9:37 PM EDT

Mr. LaFond,

I have also read Musashi - maybe three times - but his advice has to be adapted to modern America; yours doesn't.

The Logic of Steel is, for me, a modern Book of Five Rings/Spheres. Better still, in 2012, you wrote "Managing Violence." At age 61, I'm still teaching high school. I use your advice on controlling myself, to enable me to not kill some of the students.

The kids know how to make teachers feel like Kenneth, rent-a-cop-from-hell. Your advice helps me to get around that.

As I said, please keep writing.

Mark Lawrence

responds: June 28, 2015 9:33 AM EDT

I'm, so glad The Logic of Steel was helpful for you and that you found the site.

Ironically, many knife enthusiasts dislike the book as it discourages the use of a knife for self-defense in many scenarios. Being an apostate, it's nice to have an approving mind out there on this sticky subject.

Thanks for the encouragement. I will keep writing—beginning the stick-fighting book today.

As far as Mister Kenneth, I have not seen him in 15 years. He would be about 75. His best stories are in When You're Food. My favorite is when he fights two young guys, gets his ass kicked, and then his sons and the cops show up at the same time...

Have fun with those darling school students.

James

Mark Lawrence   June 25, 2015 7:18 PM EDT

Mr. LaFond,

I have studied various styles of karate, kung-fu, etc., for 43 years - and your writings are more relevant than all the Musashi's and Sun Tzu's rolled together. Outside my home, I am always accompanied by my hickory cane, and its mere presence has prevented two potential late-night robberies and various other acts of violence. When their eyes drift down to the cane in my hand, they always go their way, rather than act.

Please keep writing.

Mark Lawrence

Phoenix, AZ

responds: June 26, 2015 4:17 PM EDT

Mark,

Thanks. I can take the Chinese philosopher or leave him. But let us honor Musashi. I have read his little book 9 times. What he basically says is that martial arts are for sissies. Check out the article Little Sissy Things on the Ancient Combat page—one of my first posts from 2012, I think.
Thanks for the encouragement. It really matters.

'How Do You Deal With Aggression?'

A Man Question from Mira

"James, thanks for the stick advice. That was very helpful.

"How do you deal with aggression? I understand that you have fighting skills, and your manipulative conversation tricks to manage encounters with unpleasant people. With me being a woman, I understand we are made of different stuff. But how do you deal with the corrosive internal affects of being in aggressive situations with negative people?

"This is something that I've only really been able to deal with through isolating myself. I could not imagine being able to stay level under the circumstance you seem to thrive in. I have to consider, however, in light of the deteriorating nature of our world, that I might find myself among crowds of negative people one day. How do you maintain your peace of mind with the people you are in contact with? Do you have any tips specific for a pink collar woman?

Mira

Mira, to put it bluntly, if you had a big bony fist and invasive genitalia this would be far easier to walk you through.

Women seek connectivity with those around them, which gives them the wrong type of sensitivity—which, to a fighter is like intelligence to the military—for dealing with external adversarial aggression. The type of aggression women thrive on and which is corrosive to the man's peace of mind, is in-group bonding and bickering, once typified by home living dominated by females, and now typified by day care, school environments, and most workplace situations.

This is why women, in all traditional societies, stayed home, and men went out to hunt. To the extent that a man becomes acclimated to the in-group stresses of our collective home, school and work spaces, he will be less capable of handling the predatory out-group stresses I often write about.

Mira, the more you need acceptance, belonging, comfort, warmth, gratitude, the more vulnerable you will be out in the world of crime, and the more harried you will be in your workplace, particularly if you find yourself working with aggressive and negative persons who may have come from the world of crime and aggression. Indeed, the Baltimore City Council is working on—and may have passed—a bill that will make criminal background checks of prospective employees illegal. Imbedding criminals in the work force anonymously, when it happens, will go further towards cultivating the type of hostile world you seem concerned about facing one day.

Postmodern Social Stress Factors

The following will increase your stress.

-You are intelligent enough to perceive things that most people do not. Extensive unsuccessful boxing could go some way towards remedying this.

-You care about people in general and have a strong sense of humanity—prepare to suffer! That is why I am a live and let die kind of guy. I regard most humans as mindless animals undeserving of my time, let alone my care.

-You are a member of a group that does not have strong tribal markers, such as rituals, and priorities that go beyond the material concerns of making a buck. Someone who belongs to a biker gang will have more peace of mind than someone on a Wal-Mart shift. By this definition most workplace and all compulsory schooling environments are toxic to the human soul.

-Your identity is dependent on the approval of others. If you are a member of a tribal group and you are subject to group approval, you are in balance, have achieved a give and take with your group. However, if your identity—the seat of your peace of mind—hinges on the approval of others, and you are in a typical school or workplace environment, prepare to suffer. The strength of the tribe is that it cultivates the need for approval in stringent ways, and rewards that need. The workplace setting uses our tribal wiring against us, to reduce us to a cipher. In order to remain in balance in a workplace setting you must have your need for approval met outside of it, by your martial arts club, your book discussion group, etc.

Alienation as an Antidote

I have dealt with stress by voluntarily alienating myself through the disciplines of fighting and writing, which encompass the discipline of distancing oneself from society, and from others. I require solitude, and manufacture it in my mind and with my actions when it is not available.

I do often sympathize and empathize with others, but direct it into my writing, as I do with anger. I learned this through fight training. Instead of striking an insulting person, or even arguing with them, I would walk away. The next day they would be the heavy bag or the training post, or the barbell, or any training apparatus, even my shadow on the block wall of the gym.

I highly recommend adopting two arts: one physical, one cerebral and creative, as avenues for stress relief, and to recycle stress into something good or useful.

Spiritual disciplines help make space between you and the maddening noise of this unnatural world. When I have fought or sparred or trained I feel as if resurrected from a suffocating, incomplete death. While much of the interactive mechanics I use to manage aggression and its impact on my soul have more to do with writing than fighting, it is the physical art that offers up the transcendent experience. Many people may have the opposite orientation. Find out what your orientation is.

As for being a woman, I would suggest that, contrary to the wisdom of our late great philandering nuclear die-rolling president, J.F.K., who famously said, "No man is an island," I heartily disagree. In my cracked mind the only man, and the only woman—the only human being worthy of the appellation that supposedly raises us above the status of a mere primate animal—capable of transcending the miserable condition prepared for us by our masters, is, and must be, an island.

Mira, your island might be "a fortress of solitude" or merely the spiritual equivalent of the grassy medium of a busy highway. Your island might not be my hairy haunted battle matrix—and may very possibly be a knitting chair—but it needs to have a shoreline, so you know when the water is rising.

I am unqualified to comment on woman-to-woman stress. As far as dealing with men, you have to learn how to spot the honorable ones at a glance. My best advice for lone women is to form a moral bond with honorable men, and not to get too manipulative about it, so that you will have someone to call on in a pinch, especially the kind of pinch Baltimore experienced this past April. In the meantime that skill of recognizing honorable men—which means they will respect you even though you are weaker than they—can be used to sift through the masculine rubble of our current male population while out and about in order to avoid the bad, associate with the good, and forget about all of the worthless steer meat in between.

Maureen   June 27, 2015 10:01 PM EDT

That last comment was mine James...thanks.

 **responds:** June 28, 2015 9:13 AM EDT

Thank you, Maureen.

Anonymous   June 27, 2015 10:01 PM EDT

"The more you need acceptance, belonging, comfort, warmth, gratitude, the more vulnerable you will be out in the world of crime, and the more harried you will be in your workplace, particularly if you find yourself working with aggressive and negative persons who may have come from the world of crime and aggression."

Boy you nailed it. I was in a little office of 4 women, Two White, one African, One Mex Mix. The other White woman (from Eastern Europe), just kept her nose to the grindstone. I did too but the "minority sisters" picked up on my neediness pretty quickly and used it to play games with my head. I left that job after 6 months.

I'm trying to learn to deal with these kinds of things in this messed up world. I need money!

responds: June 28, 2015 9:12 AM EDT

That need for money is placed there by our society to keep us at the mercy of others.

It is much tougher to break that need for a woman on a few counts.

I wish you luck. In the meantime, take that Eastern European chick's lead. Even if you fake it, not seeming to care brings power when it comes to dealing with workplace aggression.

Any type of work, like landscaping or house cleaning, where you only have to take crap from the person that is also giving you the money, is better, has more balance.

I know dozens of people, right now, in your predicament. You can find the crease in the negativity matrix and slip through. It just takes time and diligence.

A View of Our Infrastructure

Notes From A Rural Water Management DRC

In light of the resent unrest in my hometown I have been more curious about our nation's infrastructure. For instance, what if the few hundred hoodrats who fought the Baltimore Police Department to a standstill and looted over 200 business and set over 150 fires, targeted local utilities instead? What would that be like? A friend of mine works for a rural water utility. Below are some notes and observations he gave me to post on the site.

I have about 30 years experience: 15 in water, 15 in wastewater.

We have 3 operators on call for 6,000 customers, serving about 14,000 men, women and children.

There are 6 total DRC for on call operators, DRC is acronym for Direct Responsible Charge, our schedule is 8/6 rotation. We are licensed by the state at different levels. I'm grade 4 water treatment, grade 4 water distribution, grade 3 wastewater treatment. We have to complete 30 credit hours of CEUs to keep our certification. This is over a three year renewal. CEU is continuing education units. If you screw up big time they take your certification and you are out of a job.

I just finished my 8 day on call marathon, with a 24 hour binge starting on Monday morning and ending today at noon. We had a power outage. A dumbass drove a boom truck under a power line. Because the power systems are at full throttle any outage forces other grids to pick up the slack. It causes what I call a cascade effect. We experience immediate power drops as the system tries to compensate. If you are a water operator it kicks out the motors running the water distribution system so they don't single phase, burning them up.

I was thinking about the e-mail I sent you about a nationwide outage, one truck, affected half the county for 24hrs. This also burns out the small components of our SCADA system, which created the nightmare: 2 lone operators; 2 rednecks overseeing water sources for 14,000 people, kind of funny don't you think?

Based on the fact that the police departments and political leadership of Baltimore City and Baltimore County, simultaneously declined to protect the citizenry, and devoted all assets to protecting key government officials and buildings and upscale residential enclaves, I consider it likely that real terrorists, if they really exist in the virulent numbers we are led to believe, might take such events in the future as cues to attack utilities, which would go a long way towards expanding your own personal Boned Zone if you happened to live in the affected area.

Relevant Links

https://en.wikipedia.org/wiki/SCADA

http://www.bing.com/news/search?q=Scada&qpvt=scada&FORM=EWRE

Wearing Glasses in a Street Fight?

A Man Question from Dominick

"I know you wear glasses. What would you do about that if you had to fight?"

Dominick Mattero, 7/28/15

I require glasses for reading beyond 18 inches. I take them off to read a book and put them on to write or read on the computer. On the street they are only good for reading bus headers and street signs, and I often switch to sunglasses now since my brain is melting down and causing my most damaged eye to become sensitive to light.

I have been hit while not looking while wearing my glasses and they did not damage me and survived themselves as they flew from my face. An up jab or knee to the eye could turn the lens into an eye-injuring device. It is most likely that they would just fly from the face if hit by most strikes. There is also a chance that they could protect your eyes, from an eye poke, gouge, mace [just a reduction], thrown bleach, spit, hot coffee, or tossed grit, all of which have been used as weapons by and against friends of mine in Baltimore.

Tactically, the glasses are beneath consideration—with any concern for them being the kind of materialistic quibbling that a woman would engage in.

If I am ambushed the glasses, if they become a concern, become an immediate liability.

If I have decided to launch a preemptive strike and take my glasses off than I have just shown my hand.

Even if you are nearly blind without the glasses losing them is not a big deal. One of the best boxers I ever worked with just saw shadows and he was a monster. If he sees a human shadow he knows where the nose and the liver are. He's human after all.

Keep in mind how vulnerable the eyes are. The toughest fighters in the world become babies in a split second when poked in the eye. Glasses will protect against most street fighting and survival situation eye abrasions. My oldest son just had both of his corneas burned on the job. A simple pair of glasses might have saved him.

There is a type of punch that will turn the glasses into an eye-shredding weapon. But if the dude can throw that punch and hits you with it, then it's your fault for getting in a time machine and fighting Hen Pearce in the London Prize Ring.

Most of all, the pitfall of taking even a split second of combat thought and devoting it to your glasses, is that if your antagonist attacks at that moment you are at a tactical disadvantage. Your antagonist deserves all of your attention for at least so long as it takes to put him down. Give it to him. He's earned it.

O Hayes   July 29, 2015 10:41 PM EDT

"If he sees a human shadow he knows where the nose and the liver are. He's human after all." That was probably the best thing I've read all month. I read an article yesterday about 2 new species of pseudoscorpions being discovered in the caves of the Grand Canyon. They adapted to cave dwelling so well that they no longer need eyes so they evolved without them and now hunt and strike vital areas of prey purely by 'ear' and instinct.

 **responds:** July 30, 2015 10:50 AM EDT

Oliver, I am very pleased that my Nobel Nominated article on fighting with glasses on has met with your approval.

What is more, imagine the thrill I felt when I discovered that my prize boxer, who I have touted as a possible MMA match for Bruce Lee in his prime, who has not been out to train for two weeks, is using that muscular posterior carved by the very hand of God from rarest ebony, to sit on while he watches films about scorpions!

Jeremy Bentham   July 29, 2015 12:32 PM EDT

Fortunately nowadays the lens on most eyeglasses are made of some sort of shatterproof plastic rather than glass as they were in years past. http://www.webmd.com/eye-health/eyeglasses-eyes. Wearing protective eyewear is even mandatory for U.S. soldiers in combat now. They even make protective eyeglasses with little magnifying inserts for us old folks who need reading glasses now. Pretty handy!

Way back in the mid 70's I saw someone get seriously hurt in a karate tournament when he got kicked in the face while wearing eyeglasses. It was a black belt match, one competitor nailed the other squarely between the eyes with the instep of his right foot in a textbook roundhouse kick. The kick alone was enough to knock the daylights out of the unfortunate recipient and from where I stood I could see that the blow shattered one of the lens of his eyeglasses and had driven pieces into his eye. He staggered briefly with blood running down his face and then collapsed in a heap. The prostrate man was quickly swarmed by officials and medics and was taken off the mat. Naturally the 64,000 dollar question is why was this man, a black belt and presumably an experienced competitor, wearing glasses in a karate tournament? Well the rules mandated no contact to the face, so I must guess that he figured that would protect him. Oh well. Had the man been wearing eyeglasses with modern polycarbonate lenses, he could have been confident that not only would they not shatter from a blow, but that they could even stop birdshot fired from a shotgun at some distance.

responds: July 30, 2015 1:15 PM EDT

That story is one for the archives. Thanks Jeremy.

To this day, facial contact is often forgiven in the black belt division at karate tournaments, as long as no blood is drawn.

Purge?

A Man Question from Adam

"James, I thought you coined [as an urban American activity] the term purge. But in one of your recent Harm City posts you quoted a hood rat using the term. Do you have readers among the hood rat population?"

Thanks Adam, I suppose this is as good a time to classify the term as any.

I first became aware of the term in March by watching a pair of horrible Left wing movies about rich right wingers hunting poor blacks while other rich centrists hide in gated enclaves. For what it's worth, the second movie is far better than the first.

I next heard the term, a month later, from Miss Ezz, the Ghetto Grocress, that her store was being targeted by the students of Frederick Douglas High School and three gangs, for a 'Purge' which was taken to mean a hunt for white people combined with looting and destruction.

The Boned Zone

The chief of Police, Uncle Tom Bighouse, repeated this term to the national press—quoting it directly off of hood rat social media—and was later disciplined for using this term.

The media discarded the term used by the purgers to accurately describe what they were doing.

The media also declined to report any and all accounts of attacks on whites by purging blacks.

The media elected instead, in lockstep with government, to call the activity 'rioting.'

The media has since softened the terminology to 'unrest' and now stands two full steps removed from the truth.

Since then I have heard the term used four times: twice by hood rats casually discussing planned activities, undoubtedly actually consisting of finger-painting for charity at the Special Olympics venue along with poster children from Saint Jude's Children's Hospital.

There is also, in the back of my mind, the memory of an innocent unarmed black youth saying that he was "goin' to purge your ass." I do not recall if that was said to me or someone else.

Also, still nestled in the partially undamaged frontal lobe of my brain, is the memory of a thug mumbling to the police that he and his friends would "purge" if any arrests were made at the food store I work at. This account can be found in *The America That Liberals Want*.

So far, only black youth have used this term outside of the filmmakers who seemingly inspired their heroics.

As for what the purge means, and the form it will take on in Baltimore again and again [for we have had numerous small purges since the main event at the end of April] it is viewed in the minds of the people who coined the term and live by it, as a means to exact social vengeance on white people by harming individual whites in gang attacks, and at the same time redistribute income from any party who has earned it, including blacks, under the cover of political mayhem.

To offer a clear definition of purge, according to the black Baltimore youth who use it: "attack whites on sight and take whatever you can, from whoever you can, under cover of arson and threats upon the lives of police officers"

Purging is a sound social warfare strategy, which has worked, will be repeated, will work in the future, will become increasingly more successful, and will be adapted to be more effective as the ruling elite permits it's law enforcement personnel to slowly adapt ineffective countermeasures.

One aspect of the April purge that was well-timed was making it at the end of the month when criminally inclined poor have no remaining welfare benefits and will be easily enticed into ancillary looting which will draw the focus of the media and law enforcement way from sweat targets like pharmacies and liquor stores.

This strategy—wholly unknown and undreamed of by the liberal elite—may yet be improved upon by timing a purge for the end of a long month that leads into a month in which the 1st does not fall on the weekend. You see, this week, the mayhem at area markets intensified every day, and crescendoed yesterday with old black ladies in power chairs shoplifting in packs and breaking for the open road in a fan formation with hams and such tucked under their seats. Today, Friday, being the 31st, should have been the worst day yet, with open robberies at bus stops and shoplifting rising to the point of looting in retail outlets. However, since the 1st of August falls on a non-business day, welfare came out today.

The schedule of welfare payments are:

Cash, $250 per dependent, on the first day of the month, or the last business day before the 1st if it falls on a Saturday, Sunday or holiday

Food stamps, $250 per dependent issued alphabetically from the 6th to the 15th [soon to change to 4-24, distributed by Social Security numbers, which will cause additional clustering effects] which will place maximum ancillary unrest associated with purges from the 26th-31st of the month.]

Watch the moon Adam, and when it looms large know that whoever your local welfare recipients are, that they are primed to attack you for the twin crimes of being born white and having worked to acquire something that rightfully belongs to the Children of the State.

You will know specifically when a purge is about to kick off when there is a news report [or not] that police have been threatened by gangs on social media. Once such a threat is made the police will hunker down and leave us to our own devices. After such a warning I suggest going to war.

Adam   July 31, 2015 2:04 PM EDT
The color of my skin is not a crime, nor is it a crutch. I will watch the moon and ready myself, lest I be caught unawares. Should that become the case, then let the weak fall.

'Not Raping Mel Gibson's Wife'

The Care and Feeding of The American Negro by Jacque Negro

This is the funniest Sotomayor video to date. I think I broke a rib laughing at this. Mister Sotomayor takes plenty of heat for being anti-black. But if you pay close attention you will notice he is primarily speaking out against black people doing bad things to other black people.

When I first moved to Baltimore and ended up working with a black fellow named Earl, and we decided to pitch in for crabs, he told me about a good place to get them cheap and took me there. On the way he gave me a tour of the ghetto. He drove me down this street in Sand Town [Freddie Gray's hood] and said, "Look, this is what your tax dollars are going for, fixing all of these places up for my people."

The houses did indeed look well renovated.

Earl then turned the corner and drove down another street that looked like a cross between a horror movie set and Stalingrad in 1943, and said, "And this is what my people are going to turn those houses into. Three years ago this block looked like that block. Three years from now this block will look like that block—welcome to Baltimore."

https://www.youtube.com/watch?v=ThtRGNQAsnU

'Uncle Tom's Ghost'

Since the Termination of Harm City Police Chief Uncle Tom Bighouse Homicides are at All-time High

...and the negro wench in charge of the Baltimore kitchen is getting help from her white federal daddy...

The BPD Homicide clearance rate is a cheering 36%!

With 45 Harm Citizens slain in July, the 1972 all-time high has been matched, and per capita, exceeded, as we have 275,000 fewer residents.

On one night 10 people were shot, but only one killed, reflecting a strong trend toward non-lethal shootings indicative of new gang war players. Hopefully hood rat marksmanship soon improves to the point that most shootings are lethal. Two of these hoodrats limped into an emergency room with bullets in them for the second time this year!

No previous year has had two months with more than 40 killings, and we've already crushed that.

The Boned Zone

The May through July number of slain is 116, also unsurpassed or matched in the city's sordid past.

Ten federal pigs from various agencies have been brought in to help solve murders.

These ten goons will join 20 ATF pigs already on the ground in Baltimore.

I predicted federal policing in Baltimore when the DOJ pressured the mayor to order her pigs to stand down. The federal fanning and stoking of the violence in Baltimore was an obvious ploy to spread the tentacles of the police state. Other small and mid-sized cities will see federal pressure on local police to stand down in the face of media-cultivated racial hysteria, followed by "boots on the ground" [this military term is now being used by law enforcement officials in Baltimore] federal intervention. It will be interesting to observe how extensive and accelerated this trend will be.

I am thrilled. The next time the BPD stands down in the face of unruly teens and men fan out in packs to hunt the streets of Baltimore for people like me while the media declines to report this loudly proclaimed purging activity by black gangs, I will be comforted to know that a federal expert will be on hand to investigate the aftermath.

The stage that follows on that will be grunt level federal police on the streets. I expect to see the U.S. Marshal's Service expanded to fill this role. In the meantime I'm fascinated by the developments, and hope that Uncle Tom Bighouse is fishing somewhere off a quiet country pier, far away from the urban war he was not permitted to fight, and was then blamed for losing.

A police chopper has been over my home for the past 15 minutes and is making low passes over by the local pre-penitent—I mean school. At least four times daily a BPD helicopter is making passes over my neighborhood in search patterns, always accompanied by frenzied pig-mobile deployments.

You can get your Harm City tourist brochures at the kiosk at Highland Avenue and Baltimore Street.

PR   August 4, 2015 11:00 PM EDT

"federal expert" - Oxymoron spotted.

Increased Junky Violence

In the Aftermath of the Late April Purge in Baltimore

Up until the purge of late April it was common, in the suburban working class supermarket I work in, for one of the lowlife stoners, junkies, food-stampers, shoplifters or whores to threaten an employee about once per week. Since the beginning of May we have seen on average of five threats per a week. I'm confident that I am not undercounting as threats are reported from employee to employee religiously. Management tends to distance itself from customer on employee threats in most retail food operations, and this one is no exception. Employees don't even bother telling management any longer. As with filling out a police report it is an exercise in futility.

There has been a much reduced police presence in this neighborhood beginning at exactly the same time. It has gotten bad enough that I have informally offered my assistance to my direct supervisor, as I saw more of this kind of action in a day in the city market I once managed than he is accustomed to seeing in a month. In fact he has been repeatedly threatened by male shoplifters, stalkers [of shemale (a typo, and I'm keeping it!) staff] pimps, and panhandlers.

This morning at 4:18 I emerged from the stockroom with a u-boat of yogurt as one 20 year old punk with brown curls walked by with two whipped topping canisters. His gauged, pierced, tattooed and barefoot grunge-hippie friend then addressed me, "Hey, Brother where is the whipped cream."

Knowing he was going to snort it, but assuming he would pay for it after asking for it, I directed him and watched him float off upon clouds of intoxication. Ten minutes later the night captain brought two canisters back over, told me he caught the kid beginning to huff it—the other kid had already huffed his and we found those ditched behind the noodles an hour later—and that he caught the two girls who entered with the two guys stealing no-dose pills.

As he walked the red-handed thieves out, the brown curled huffer boasted to the cashier, Bubba, as he accompanied his friends, "If you accuse me of stealing I'm punching you in the face."

The night captain, asked me for a rundown on how I used to deal with this stuff, and after I told him, he related the following, "We used to fine them fifty bucks, they pay or we take them to court, but they don't pay. You take them to court –which necessitates paying one of us to spend a half day in court—and as soon as they open their mouth and tell the judge they have a substance abuse problem he's like, 'Oh, son you already have enough problems to deal with,' and throws it out. He won't do anything unless we catch them hauling off a truck load.

"They can swear at you, threaten you, hit you, steal from you, bust up your store and the judge says, 'Do you expect me to lock them up for stealing a gallon of milk?'

" 'Well, yes!'

"I said, 'Your Honor, what do you expect us to do, just let them take what they want, or should we cut off a finger?'

"Well, he didn't want to hear that. That was it for me at the courthouse. We stopped wasting our time in court. Now I just block their way out and tell them they're not getting past me until they empty their hands and pockets. And now the threats—everybody wants to punch you in the nose—and if I touch them back it's my job, my ass—a law suit. This world is just upside down.

Everything I was ever taught about right and wrong does not apply anymore."

As far as I can tell there is a direct correlation with threats against staff and the near total absence of police on the property and in the vicinity, where previous to the April purge the officers of this precinct were high profile crime fighters. The cops now generally limit themselves to enforcing traffic violations on the primary road.

PR   August 4, 2015 11:04 PM EDT

"The cops now generally limit themselves to enforcing traffic violations on the primary road."

What men! Have any of these worthies tendered their resignations since they're obviously returning no value to the taxpayer, or will they continue to draw a paycheck as their fair city becomes rubble?

Harm City Homeboycides

Baltimore's Most Eugenic Month on Record Closes with the Death of "G-Rock"

The so-called black community is finally bemoaning the black-on-black slaughter [apparently marking the extended celebration of Freddie Gray's death] since the death of 29 year-old rapper Donte "G-Rock" Dixon at the close of July.

Last Sunday a youth councelor told me that the girl who was raped, tortured, murdered and burned in my neighborhood was at fault for her own death for associating with boys in a gang. It did not seem to occur to him that she most likely did not request death by vaginal impalement with a sharpened broomstick. There you go, according to a churchgoing family man, if a girl dates a criminal she deserves to be horribly murdered.

In any case, the only blacks that blacks seem to grant agency to remain victims—and Denzel Washington—with all other blacks in America faultless, with blame for their actions diverting by default to the black victim or faceless white daddy.

On the other hand, if I kill someone it is my fault. And these people do not realize that they are elevating me far above the moral plane upon which they place their own kind—except, of course for the victims of black-on-black murder, who magically become the moral equivalent of the Whiteman!

Well, when a black entertainer is killed people seem to wake up.

So far here is Baltimore's eugenic homicide scorecard, with ties broken according to per capita ratio:

#5-August 1990: 42

#4-May 2015: 42

#3-December 1971: 44

#2-August 1972: 45

#1-July 2015: 45

Yo, I be kina OCD. So do yo think we could off 43 homeboys in August so that this makes a nice stair-step bar-graph for the print version?

Your Blazing Chariot

Notes on the Rolling Urban Deathtrap for Surviving the Purges to Come

Apollo Helios blazed across the skies of myth in his flame-wheeled chariot and his sisters the Heliads turned to trees and cried amber tears when he met with tragedy. Ever since our kind first enslaved the horse, winging across the world in a conveyance of one kind or another has obsessed us. Even though I am a lowly pedestrian I have written numerous fantasies centered on the power complex that is Man's relationship with the automobile. As with many aspects of our complex society it is part reality and part delusion.

From Cart to Car

The car is the direct lineal descendent of the chariot. Like the modern car the ancient chariot was used for war, racing, and the ceremonial procession of dignitaries. Unlike the car, it was not an everyday method of transportation.

The Boned Zone

The most famous conjoined twins in history, the Sons of Aktor, raced against Herakles in a chariot.

Achilles was brought to the battlefield and set down to rage across it via chariot.

Ramses was driven across the battlefield in a chariot, feathering foes with his composite bow.

Caesar was paraded in his triumph aboard a chariot.

Be warned though, from the groaning depths of sorrowful antiquity, the Sons of Aktor were mangled, and chariot racing was far more deadly for the driver than boxing was for the boxer. Consider, also, that Achilles did not drive his chariot, but rode in, and then dismounted and speared the lowly chariot drivers that served rival heroes with cruel impunity. Consider that Ramses' favorite targets were the drivers of his enemy warlords. Be mindful also, that the war chariot was eventually driven from the battlefield by the lowly, lightly armed, foot soldier.

This lesson has echoed down through the ages.

Did Napoleon drive his carriage?

Did Rommel drive his staff car, or was he driven by an enlisted man?

Did Ike, Patton or Macarthur drive their jeeps, or did some disposable GI do it for them?

Cars in Urban America

The modern car may be used as a weapon—either a bomb or battering ram—but remains a light transportation device, a veritable deathtrap for its occupant. And, if you choose to use it as a weapon, your are still nothing more than the software, the guidance system.

The timeless lesson of the light transport's vulnerability was clearly illuminated when the Baltimore City Police Department and the Maryland Transit Authority Police lost numerous vehicles to teens less well-armed than the barbarian infantry that drove the chariot from the battlefield in early antiquity. Indeed some MTA police are now taking legal action against the State of Maryland for not protecting them against the children of Baltimore City! One of their vans—which we might as well call a pussy wagon—is pictured burning as our Baltimore Travel Guide Icon on this site.

I personally have, in the streets, alleys and lots of Baltimore, been attacked, chased, and stalked from such automobiles numerous times, and have successfully defeated my enemies with a stone, a pipe, a brick, a hammer, a tomahawk—I kid you not, and those were two scared-ass hoodlums—a razor blade, a utility knife, and my lonely brain.

When some asshole in a car follows you down an alley at night and discovers that you have a brick and he needs to execute a K-turn while you cave his window and head in, then he is prone to surrender and even apologize for trying to run you over for firing him.

Perhaps my most memorable moment in consideration of the vulnerability of motorists in stopped cars was when I was walking north on Belair Road in 1992 with Mike, a crack dealer who had been working the corner across the street from the clothing store in Harlem where "Iron" Mike Tyson broke his hand on Mitch "Blood" Green's face, when the non-fight went down. I had made this walk many a time and had been attacked and threatened by blacks. Mike, a black dude, told me that with him there I was probably safe from his brothers, but that now we had to worry about having the police called on us. Still a little naïve about the police and my fellow whites, I questioned him. Then, as we crossed Frankford Avenue before a dozen or so cars stopped at the light, he whispered, "Listen!" and it sounded like popcorn popping as all of those white people locked their car doors.

The Boned Zone

So, while seated within our magical plastic carpets, our ape brains do, at some level, process the fact that we are just sitting on our ass next to a potential attacker on foot. But for most of us our materialistic peasant yearning to be the big powerful man in the car overcomes us and we feel like the king of the road while it is moving around, forgetting that the only people who are worthy of the royal attribution in this world are passengers, with some peasant schmuck carting them around.

I have often been in automobiles with people who are not in any way effective combatants, who, while sitting in a light conveyance, will break bad with obvious criminals. Most of the time my rage at the driver for getting me in a fight at a traffic stop is mistaken by the other road raging asshole as intent to do harm and they speed off. Only one driver spared me, a girl named Megan, who I was dating when three red necks in a pickup cussed her out. She ignored them and then said, after they passed, "I wouldn't do that to you. They just wanted me to give them an excuse to kick your ass."

Megan, to date, is the only driver I have ridden with who understands that if they mouth off and get caught at a stop, than I, the passenger, will have to do the fighting.

The Purge Mobile

Until the Mondawmin Riots in April cops felt invincible one to a car. Then, when the riots kicked off one of the first film shots was of a handful of rock-armed hoodrats driving one pig from his car, a pig who all of a sudden found himself in the twig hut with wolves at the door. To resist the hoodrat offensive the cops had to dismount, just as war fighters do in urban environments when they don't want to get roasted alive in their unarmored vehicles.

The only effective police use of vehicles was by the tactical squad who—even though they had an armored vehicle—walked beside it and used it as a mobile base of operations, not as a refuge.

As for motorists, 8-year-old hoodrats were stopping them with barricades made of dropped bicycles!

When I discuss cars as deathtraps I am not talking about Hummers, jacked up steel-frame Jeeps and monster pickup trucks. These are what you want as a minimum if you want to consider driving through enemy territory during a purge. In rural and suburban environments a car often offers a huge advantage. But in a built up urban area with hostiles on foot a car is a deathtrap, small pickups as well. The key thing to consider is where your head is as you sit behind that panel of light glass, at the height of the attacker's hips, where his maximum force may be applied to whatever he is doing. I have spoken to large men who have dragged drivers out through windows. Then there is the vulnerability of trying to get out under duress, of standing under someone while they can kick the door shut on your shins.

Saving Your Ass On Wheels

Below I offer a minimum of advice for the motorist in an urban purge environment. I also encourage our online military readers to offer additional tips, or correct me, based on your experience operating light vehicles in urban threat zones.

1. Do not drive alone. The cops got jacked up back in April so bad because they were used to hunting fleeing individuals by using multiple single occupant cars to converge on their prey and then dismount and pursue on foot. For the month of May cops buddied up, which is the only sensible thing to do, and the military contractors—who actually know what the hell they are doing—drove 4 to a car. The Baltimore Pig Dee has

since dispersed its officers one to a vehicle again, making them ripe for the next purge.

2. The most qualified combatant should be the passenger. Have your wife drive—hell that's the only time white women get aggressive enough to be scary is when they are behind the wheel. Use that.

3. The passenger should have a short crowbar or tire iron or heavy flashlight at hand and be prepared to kick the door into the knees of anyone getting too close before braining them with the weapon. Someone is going to use that door as a weapon, and it might as well be you, cracker. *The BPD chopper is hovering over my house again. When this shit breaks loose again it's going to be nasty.*

4. If there is a second combatant—who is only viable if this is a 4-door—place him behind the driver.

5. If you seriously expect to be in a position where you will have to drive through a purge zone, buy a hockey helmet with face cage—if it's good enough for the PBR [Professional Bull Riders] it's good enough for you— and keep it handy.

6. Do not, ever, go into an American city low on gas. Never use city gas pumps.

7. Keep a pair of safety glasses handy to put on incase of trouble.

8. Never, ever drive through an urban environment with windows down, or even cracked.

9. The passenger side door is the favored entrance point for a carjacker. Make sure yours is always locked.

10. If you are ever bumped by another car in an urban center, and you do not judge yourself capable of defeating the occupant[s] of that vehicle in hand-to-hand combat do not leave your vehicle to exchange information, but call the police and wait—forever most likely. The cops actually want you to be carjacked exchanging information rather than referee the thing when they could be making their monthly ticket quota.

11. In a stop situation the passenger-combatant, should call the shots, not the driver. Tell your girl, your wife, your son, your dad behind the wheel that when anything goes down and you are in the passenger seat that you are calling the shots, as your range of vision and tactical response will be better, and also not impeded by involvement with operating the machine.

12. If you have a woman behind the wheel who won't melt down immediately, she is still likely to go stupid

under stress and not be able to make decisions. So you should rehearse basic commands ahead of time. One word commands such as 'reverse,' 'turn,' 'u-turn,' 'stop' and 'go' should be made by you and obeyed when the stress level amps up.

13. Between the passenger seat and the door should be a steel extension weapon, such as a crowbar, a crowbar, or a crowbar, for use by the combatant in a dismount situation.

Ideally, for any trip through an urban purge zone, you have a mean little dude behind the wheel, a big aggressive guy armed with a tire iron and a crowbar in the passenger seat, and a vicious knife-armed creep seated behind the driver. If this seems crazy, imagine you are at work, you and three other motorists. To get through a purge zone and out of town you are better off all piling into the most durable 4-door car, or the biggest goddamned truck. Perhaps you drove to work and two co-workers did not. There is your foot support right there. Put the dishwasher in the passenger seat with a frying pan and the cook in the back seat with his butcher knife.

In a sane world it would be three decent men with firearms. But in most cities where purges are likely I suspect the government has already curtailed the rights of citizens to carry firearms to the extent that not one member of most conceivable pairs or trios of everyday people are likely to have a concealed carry permit. If someone does have a gun it certainly should not be the driver. I have no handgun experience or training, so would like to ask those of you who do, to post a comment as to where the man with a handgun should be in a car occupied by three or four civilians.

During the writing of this piece, between 1 and 3 p.m., I heard three different police sirens attached to speeding cruisers roaring down my street, separated by at least 15 minutes each. There were also two search passes by the chopper, and two ambulance scrambles. My neighborhood has had more police and emergency service activity than at any time I can recall since moving here in 2010. My best friend is bringing me a bunch of food this weekend as she is abruptly leaving town without even selling her house. She's been biting at the bit to get the hell out of Harm City every since April. She is one of three personal friends of mine moving out this summer. Ajay is a doll and I will miss her, but this town is no place for a lady.

It is 3:11 as I post and the chopper is back and more sirens are screaming.

I am totally jacked up on a gallon of coffee and will be heading out this evening with my heterosexual umbrella of invincibility to research a major Poor Tour location, which should post tomorrow, 8/7/15.

Jeremy Bentham   August 11, 2015 6:08 PM EDT

James since you asked, if three people are riding in a four-door car with only one armed with a gun, the best place to position the gunner would be in the back seat. That way the "tail gunner" can shoot to both the left and right sides, through the rear window and even partially cover the front without risking hitting either the driver or the front passenger. One of the problems that will arise if the front passenger, the "shotgun rider", is the only one with a gun is that he will not be able to fire his gun out the left side windows without touching it off right in front of the driver's or rear passenger's face. That will at least temporarily blind, deafen and stun them if they aren't wearing eye and ear protection. The only way for the shotgun rider to avoid doing this when engaging targets on the left would be to shoot over the top of the roof, which of course will expose him to attack in a number of ways. The best kind of motor vehicle to have in such a situation will be one with a turret or a sun roof that will allow the gunner to stand up and cover all sides of the vehicle and then duck down behind cover when objects are hurled at him or shots are fired at him. The down side is that an open sun roof can leave you vulnerable to having bricks, firebombs or grenades tossed into the passenger compartment of your vehicle, so be wary of that. Besides the hockey/lacrosse helmets and the safety glasses it will be a good idea for everyone in the car to be wearing earplugs if you expect to be firing guns from inside. It is very likely that the muzzle of a gun will be close to someone's ear when it is fired from inside the car during the chaos of battle. You will not believe how loud and how painful it will be to have a gun go off near you in a confined compartment. The cheap disposable foam earplugs will be good enough to protect you and you can easily buy enough for everyone. The Sonic or 3m Peltor Combat Arms ear plugs, while much more expensive, will be better for individual purchase since they shut out only the loud damaging noises and allow you to hear normal speech clearly. Naturally if you have Kevlar body armor it would be a real good idea to wear it while taking a Sunday drive through the combat zone.

For further study check out the 1986 Miami Massacre. It serves as a pretty good catalogue of many of the things that can go wrong when firing guns from inside moving or stationary civilian cars. Like when the veteran FBI agent who was the best shot on the team got his glasses knocked off his face when his car collided with the perp's vehicle which apparently impaired his ability to hit what he was shooting at in the ensuing gun battle. To be fore warned is to be fore armed.

https://en.wikipedia.org/wiki/1986_FBI_Miami_shootout

http://www.bing.com/videos/search?q=miami+massacre+1986&FORM=VIRE3#view=detail&mid=DE076931C05E338773ECDE076931C05E338773EChttp://www.bing.com/videos/search?q=miami+massacre+1986&FORM=VIRE3#view=detail&mid=DE076931C05E338773EC DE076931C05E338773EC

Bayonet   August 8, 2015 4:09 PM EDT

Why do you specify a crowbar for the side passenger, and a knife for the passenger behind the driver?

responds: August 8, 2015 6:30 PM EDT

If someone yanks the driver out of the car you're screwed, and I say that prick needs to lose a kidney ASAP. The knifer behind the driver is the guy that saves the driver from grappling attacks by slicing off fingers, slashing wrists and necks or stabbing.

If you are not highly trained in the use of a blunt extension weapon the crowbar is the longest, hardest, bone-crunching tool that you will be able to use without swinging it and with minimal risk of being disarmed. It is a tool and not classified as a weapon.

The simplest tool for most people to effectively use as a weapon is a claw hammer, but this is not a good weapon for avoiding the clinch against larger people.

The common item that people tend to think of first is the baseball bat, which is a terrible weapon if you are smaller or outnumbered.

Also, the crowbar is effective against cars. My roommate and training partner in 2013, Erik, used a crowbar to scarp cars for a salvage yard. It only took him 2 hours to turn a Buick into parts and scrap. The passenger is ideally your big strong aggressive guy and it would fall to him and whoever else was on the passenger side to remove obstacles.

'The Types of Kicks Used?'

A Man Question from Sean about KO's and Martial Arts Kicks in Survival Situations

"I was rereading Don't Get Boned and your statistics on kickers who inflicted KO's on their opponents intrigued me. Do you remember the types of kicks used (rear leg roundhouse, lead leg switch, front push, spinning back etc.) and do you have any recommendations for those of us who may find ourselves in the boned zone who prefer to kick as opposed to throwing with our hands?"

-Sean

In the November 2000 issue of TaeKwonDo Times I published Self-Defense and the Knockout: An Analysis of Real Fights. This is the piece I can find that best addresses kicking in survival situations. This was an isolation study of the 134 KO's from my initial survey of 460 violent encounters.

21% of unarmed KOs were inflicted by a significantly larger individual, mostly bouncers throwing people, and aggressors holding and hitting twerps and women.

21% of unarmed KOs were inflicted by significantly smaller individuals, mostly trained fighters, punching and kicking aggressors. The most common tactics of short men were the arching punch to the chin and the side-kick to the torso.

There are two main points to take from this:

1. Size is not a KO indicator

2. Trained fighters engaging in survival situations generally dispense with setup techniques and go directly to finishing bows.

There were two back leg round kicks, a back kick and a front kick that I recall. Most of the kick KOs were sidekicks, including one instant death in a hotel lobby, when a tall Jamaican kicked a short American black in the chest with a standing side kick.

Think about it, if 22% of smaller defenders dropped their opponents with a sidekick to the body, what do you think the tall kickers did? That's right, cut guys in half with their feet. The martial arts kick—almost always a side-kick against an approaching aggressor—

had the highest single strike KO rate in the survey, beating even guns, knives, bats and automobiles, with a 90%.

Keep in mind, though, that the greatest indicator that a person would inflict a KO was that he had a violent past, which typified 94% of successful KO artists in altercations.

Here is one example from the article:

This man earned his TaeKwonDo purple belt from an instructor of the ROK Tiger Brigade while reporting for the Army Times in Vietnam. The belt was torn from medical scrubs.

Jay, a mild mannered Tae Kwon Do master, was unlocking his car when he was threatened by a large drunk. As he turned, the man charged. Jay met his charge with a hopping sidekick to the torso. Jay sounded almost sickened as he recalled how the man's body folded around his foot. He turned and drove off as the man lay in a heap.

Since I was interviewing East Coast kickboxers who competed in the 70s and 80s, they were almost all Tae Kwon Do black belts, including the Wing Chun instructor that wrapped your ankle this past Sunday.

Keep in mind, that almost all unarmed KOs are inflicted with leg strength, whether they are punches, kicks or throws. Kicks tend to be best against a single charging opponent, with punches and poor leverage throws [by gigantic dudes] accounting for most KOs against members of groups.

Sean   August 14, 2015 8:20 AM EDT

Time to start practicing my stepping side kicks in boots again. It makes sense because whenever I have fought or boxed one of these kids they are always susceptible to body shots with the lean back lunging forward fighting style they learned from world star

Only time I ever got in trouble during a fight was allowing myself to get suckered into that and while reaching ate a huge right cross to the chin. That and I allowed them to setup. Learned my lesson that time I did.

Hos in the Hood

Another Day at The Epicenter of the Baltimore Purge

As the store manager at the Mondawmin Shoppers looked down the aisle he saw two ghetto girls duking it out. This was at 11:00 a.m. this morning. When the customers in his store are not threatening staff, arguing with management or stealing, they are going at it.

The combatants were 16 to 18 years old, and "on the lean side. Not big fat mammas. If they are not hanging out of their spandex yet they can't be more then eighteen."

The one young lady had purple hair. As she cussed and clawed and traded thudding punches with the other wench, her baby, perhaps eight months old, was seated nearby in the shopping cart, easily close enough to be knocked over, "screaming its little head off—scared to death."

The police officer on duty—who is required to keep the store from erupting into a total war zone—was a female. She went back to the aisle, took one look at the two girls vigorously duking it out, and retreated, calling for backup. As Butch called this into me additional police cars were arriving.

Since police officers may no longer use weapons to make an arrest of a black person, or even use force greater than that used by the criminal, there is really no way left to resolve violent situations but to let them continue until overwhelming numbers of cops are on hand. This is becoming an even more pronounced problem with people under 18 of any race. Parents are so ready to sue any cop or security person who dares to touch their sainted teens, that two Baltimore area retailers have adopted a hands off policy concerning teens:

1. Teens acting out violently and committing crimes shall not be opposed by staff or management.

2. Teen shoplifters may not be stopped or detained.

3. No shoplifter, strong armed robber, purse snatcher, or looter will have charges brought against them by the retailer.

4. Retailer personnel who have received a summons to testify in court against a criminal who was arrested on

company property by a police officer, are being verbally discouraged from appearing in court.

This is the America that Liberals want—only they don't live with it, but in their elven palaces in Rivendale.

Harm City Hoodrats in the Hunt!

Baltimore's Standout Triple-A Team has Hit 211 Homeboys Out Of The Park This Year, Equaling 2014's Year-End Total

With new hitters coming up through the farm system, the Harm City Hoodrats are poised to qualify for the World Are-you-Serious-Bitch National Title. Despite the good news, tourist bookings to Baltimore area hotels are down more than 9%.

Riddle me this, what's the matter with you people?

The seats are free. You just need to take care of your travel, food and lodging.

The majority of the homeboy hits have been scored this summer, since the student body of Frederick Douglas High School came out for spring training and raised the bar. With more than four months to go in 2015, the Harm City Hoodrats have already outscored last year's team. According to pundits we are possibly headed back to the gory days of the 1990s.

Stay tuned to jameslafond.com for updates.

Big Trippin's Myerhoff Mugging

A Negotiated Solution to Predatory Aggression

Big Trippin' is a six and a half foot tall, 25-year-old, white man, a kind of Bohemian who likes the sights and attractions of the city. He's is not a high end hipster attending elite venues like most whites who like the cultural attractions he likes. He was walking past the Myerhoff Symphony Hall when he was approached by five innocent unarmed black teens, two of which had knives. Big Trippin' also had a knife. He did not brandish it, but placed his hand on it and negotiated with the aggressors, agreeing to give up his cash, but keeping his identification and credit cards.

Personally, I could not bring myself to negotiate like this, and may well have been arrested and charged for murder. This fellow, however, took the most conservative and tactically sound course. Where most people would have put themselves at the mercy of these murderous hoodrats and some would have put themselves at the mercy of law enforcement and the media, he maintained his autonomy, and basically paid a toll.

His tactic was much the same as 18th century frontiersmen, who were often extorted into handing over portions of their haul [this happened to Daniel Boone a few times] to an aggressive group of Indians that preferred negotiation to taking out their prey at the risk of taking casualties. Of course, it is impossible for the modern human to understand that negotiations with aggressors are only possible if one is armed or perceived to be armed.

Jeremy Bentham   August 27, 2015 8:03 PM EDT

James, Massad Ayoob currently writes gun articles for the bi-monthly prepper webzine "Backwoods Home Magazine", www.backwoodshome.com. He also runs a blog on that site. Among his most useful and informative articles I think are the ones on self-defense and the law. This is really vital information for the average Joe especially since so much bad advice is promulgated on the subject. Even the advice that you sometimes get from cops and lawyers will get you locked for a long time if you were to follow it in a real situation. Like if you shoot someone on your doorstep drag him inside and put a knife in his hand. I know you have probably heard that gem before just as I have. Ayoob explains how even in Wanker County the authorities are liable to figure out pretty quickly that you altered the crime scene and then charge you with murder. The truth is usually easier to defend than a lie; at least it's not as hard to keep your story straight if you stick to what you believe to be the truth. I recommend Ayoob's recent book "Deadly Force- Understanding

Your Right to Self-Defense". It gives a much needed update on the subject from his earlier works.

Jeremy Bentham   August 21, 2015 2:11 PM EDT

"No one can negotiate without the power to compel negotiation." -Saul Alinsky, Rules for Radicals 1971 p. 119.

Very interesting! Gun writer and cop Massad Ayoob once described when he was living in NYC in the '70's how he would have a matchbook in his pocket with a ten or twenty dollar bill wrapped around it for tribute. If he got hassled by a gang of "innocent youth" he would, toss them the match book and tell them to have a round of drinks on him. He had a concealed carry permit and could have blown the miscreants all into the next experience; however since doing so would likely have complicated his life severely, he concocted this ploy in order to avoid such life altering trouble. He reported that it worked well at placating street hooligans. I supposed having a throwaway wallet with some money in it could work as well. But as you say one needs to be armed or else unusually physically imposing to pull such a negotiation off successfully.

responds: August 26, 2015 10:30 AM EDT

Ayoob was my favorite magazine writer in the 90s. Does he currently publish on a webzine that we could link to?

Nero The Pict   August 21, 2015 1:05 PM EDT

The Myerhoff and its vicinity have been the site of many muggings and in one case a few years ago the attempted scalping of a female bartender of whom I was acquainted. Some subhuman actually attacked her from behind with a hatchet. She lived.The maids and mugging delivery service has a stop near by (aka the Light Rail) also located a few blocks away is Baltimore's very own toy subway. The relative isolation and many blind spots have made this area a hunting ground for Baltimore's enterprising teens for as long as I can remember.

The attack on Big Trippin is oddly reminiscent of a similar occurrence that happened to an old Marine that was a customer of mine about 12 years ago. This event took place the next light rail stop down. Two youths approached my friend and demanded reparations. He took issue and one of the little jokers pulled a gun. They got into a scuffle and he was able to wrestle the firearm out of the hands of the little minx. He threw the pistol over a fence. He then beat feet to a safe area. His attackers were young 13-14ish? He was a big scary looking guy. Must be the lead paint....

responds: August 26, 2015 10:44 AM EDT

I have had similar accounts related to me by light rail users.

Leroy Slick

A Specialized Pillager

Big Mike just called me to inform on one of Baltimore's emerging class of professional looters.

"I've got to keep my schedule a secret, because I think this maggot has an employee informing him as to when I'll be on duty. Yesterday I caught him peeking in the front window. I made myself scarce and went into the office and waited to see him enter on the camera. No problem, right, a skinny black dude in August, wearing a beanie and a black sweatshirt?

"He doesn't do candy bars or bar soap, but goes exclusively for meat and seafood. So I had my lead. But then when I get over there, there is no one in a black sweatshirt and beanie? Then I notice this skinny black dude—they're all black around here—slinging a tenderloin under his arm and up under his shirt!

"I snagged his ass—his third arrest for shoplifting here—so they hauled him away. I don't know how long they'll hold him. But he'll be back. Next month food stamps start to get spread out, and these people have zero budgeting ability to begin with. We're going from alphabetical to social security number based distribution, meaning that a third of these people are going to make out by getting their EBT food side early, and that two thirds are going to get burned and end up waiting until the end of the month. They're going to be stealing at looting levels by this time next month."

As I hung up from speaking with Mike, the BPD chopper swooped in overhead for its first pass since last night at about midnight. My area has been the subject of chopper sweeps 3-6 times daily.

'Wasn't a Threat from the Jump'

Repentant Stoner Does Not Want Thugish Porky Pig to Do Time

The bimbo State's Attorney that in supposed to forestall the next Baltimore purge by gaining justice for Freddie Gray in court, just filed a fairly idiotic case against a white cop who shot a white criminal. Mike, a dude I have taken the bus with a few times, was looting the register at an East Baltimore ethnic grocery store at 4:30 a.m. on December 28th of 2014. At least Mike doesn't steal from his neighbors, but takes his larceny across town!

Mike is a white doper who was scrounging for drug money at a grocer near where he would cop his dope. Unfortunately somebody called the cops. He was leaving the store with $202 worth of cigarettes, $62 worth of lottery tickets and $100 in cash, which barely qualifies him for being jailed. In Baltimore, stealing less than $300 does not earn you a stay in jail unless you have no I.D. or if you say something stupid to the cops.

The Boned Zone

Mike!

Mike was heading for the side door when two pigs confronted him and popped off 15 rounds, by his count. The pigs lied and said that they had ordered him to show his hands and that he had went for his waist band—where there was nothing—according to investigators. But Mike says, "they didn't say one word," and that he "wasn't a threat from the jump."

One bullet sank into his abdomen. One bullet grazed his head and another one ricocheted off the wall and lodged in his neck. Yet another bullet went into his leg and blew out of his waist. But for all of the lead expended— and considering how much he ingested—when Mike hit the floor he didn't feel so bad. It wasn't nearly as bad as the burning sensation he felt when he got shot in the leg 25 years ago while being robbed at gunpoint.

A third officer, a meat-headed looking dude, now came to stand over him with gun drawn. Amazed that he was in so little pain, Mike looked up at the pig and said, "What did you shoot me with, a bean bag?"

The pig responded, "No, a forty-caliber, you piece of shit," and fired one round into Mike's groin.

The Boned Zone

Since Mike had had the forethought to get shot within walking distance of the world famous Johns Hopkins Trauma Center, where staff get practice plugging bullet holes in the hoodrats he buys his dope from every other day, he was saved. He emerged a month later less a spleen and short one kidney. He is now staying with his Mom up the street from me, and doesn't think that the pig should do time. He feels like an idiot for getting shot, says he's "no angel," and would just like the officer to have to apologize and perhaps lose his police job.

But the bimbo State's Attorney is looking to put Porky Pig away for life, on attempted murder and other various charges. Even if she manages to make these charges stick, all she will accomplish—since Mike is a white dude—is piss off the blacks of Baltimore that much more if she fails to get a conviction of a white officer for Freddie Gray's death. Mike actually said that he doesn't want Porky Pig to "go down the tubes," and doesn't want other officers to "hesitate to do their jobs," which makes sense, since the gun-armed black dudes that prey on stoners like him are emboldened every time a cop goes down for injuring of killing a non-compliant suspect.

However, if I were Mike's attorney, I would point out to him that all three of these cops did lie about him and falsify his arrest report, and even claimed-at one half-considered point—that Mike had been armed.

Stay tuned for another episode of As the World Swirls.

'Race Was A Factor'

3 arrests in Morell Park stabbings by Jessica Anderson and Pamela Wood

In the Thursday, August 27 issue of the Baltimore Sun, buried on the second page, is a piece of real reporting, in which the journalists got to cops on the scene and witnesses rather than consume what was being handed out by police supervisors.

On Tuesday evening, at about 6:00 p.m., on Washington Blvd., in Southwest Baltimore—which has seen a few pro fighters killed in street altercations in the past decade—there was a race-based gang fight. Outside of a liquor store that is open from 8 a.m. to 2 a.m. seven days a week, there was a group fight, which was witnessed and broken up by patrolling police officers. A group of black teens were having it out with a mixed group of white and Latino teens. The black boys had a 33 year old whore armed with a knife on their side. She stabbed 4 enemy, nearly killing one, who she stabbed near the heart. He is still in critical condition.

The Boned Zone

Even after the police broke up the fight the racial tensions continued being expressed through slurs. Getting to the officers before the higher ups could edit out the racial aspect of the altercation the babe reporters actually did some good work, even though they stuck with the teen-child narrative.

Interestingly enough, where a man who stabbed someone in the chest would draw an attempted murder or assault with a deadly weapon charge, this woman is being charged with lesser offenses.

There has been a largely unreported epidemic of knife violence in Baltimore and the surrounding county over the past year, with one EMT telling me that 1-3 stabbings a week occur in his area alone. He asked me not to name the subdivision for fear of losing his job for reporting violence that will ultimately be scrubbed from statistics.

This happened eight days before what the Bimbo Mayor and her boot-lickers are expecting to be another round of riots in response to the initial Freddie Gray hearings.

Hoodrat News Flash

Hoodrat Squealing and Darting Through Traffic For Justice Struck by Oppressormobile

I have just received a call from a witness on North Avenue and Harford Road, where the Freddie Grey Hearings are taking place [the closest court house to the scene of his fatally fatal arrest, and hence easily accessible to Sandtown hoodrats to whom he is a Jesus figure]. He informed me that a hoodrat protester was darting in and out of traffic and was struck by a car, sparking off minor violence. Another caller just informed me that the police officer that guards her facility has been diverted to the scene.

With any luck this minor riot will spark another full blown race purge and I will be attacked on my way to work tonight so that I might have a newsworthy article in the morning.

In case I have to mount a legal defense after being attacked by one of the dozens of packs of black men who, during the late April purge, hospitalized more than

14 lone white men in the very area I will be travelling through between 10 and 12 tonight, the area that has remained largely un-policed since then, I say the following in my legal defense.

I am 52, and have bad ankles—both of them currently sprained—will be carrying a backpack for my work clothes that I wear in the walk-in freezer. There is no conceivable way I can out run young men or teens. I will have to fight.

I will be walking with the aid of a handmade hickory T-cane, as this takes the burden off of my sprained ankles. I am trained in the use of a cane as a weapon, and will only use it to strike above the neck if I am outnumbered, or facing an armed attacker. Otherwise, I have every intention of inflicting limited pain and damage on the innocent, oppressed, misunderstood and inadequately empathized with Children of the State, who have simply mistaken this poor piece of aged white trash for someone who can actually afford to eat a steak dinner.

I pray to the God Queen, Hillary Goddamn Clinton, to imbue her Priestess of the Baltimore Temple with the wisdom of the Matriarchy, so that I will not be forced to commit the crime of defending myself tonight.

Amen.

The City and State Shakedown

Baltimore Mayor O'Mamma and The State of Maryland Attempt to Appease the Mob

Yesterday the family of martyred hoodrat hero and secular saint, Freddie Gray, hit the Running from the Cops Lottery, when Mayor O'Mamma awarded them $6,400,000 for the death of their role model and patriarch while in police custody. This award was announced despite the mayor's failure to acquire a $20,000,000 relief grant from the Feds.

[Update: Not surprisingly, change of venue hearings are now underway, almost immediately in the wake of the payment. The defense will certainly make the case that the BPD has proven itself unable to defeat rioters and that the six trials should be heard at a defensible venue. The City administration has just begun a delicate dance to derail the next riot.]

On a wider front, The State of Maryland—apparently readers of www.jameslafond.com –are phasing in a new food stamp distribution scheme—last week!

The Boned Zone

The FSP [Food Supplement Program], of Maryland has dispensed these benefits to crack heads and dope fiends, so that they can sell them at 50 cents on the dollar while the grandparents feed the children, between the 6th and the 15th of each month. Any idiot could have figured out that unrest planned by radicals at the end of the month can potentially pull looters who have gone without drug money for two weeks! Some geek in Annapolis was awake and did something that makes logistical sense.

In order to remedy this situation, and hopefully deny the next wave of purgers a looter smoke screen, the State is now dispersing funds between the 5th and the 19th.

From October through December drug money will be dispersed from the 4th through the 23rd.

As of January 20-16 the new drug money schedule will run from the 4th to the 27th.

The drug money used to come out according to the first letter in your last name. Now it will be dispersed according to the first three letters of your last name.

This means, that if I, a LAFond, give birth to this National Bohemian beer baby at Christmas time, that I'll receive my $250 in food stamps to feed little Sudsy on the 16th of each month.

In the interests of fairness, since I gave the Evil State a heads up on blunting riots by overfeeding the poor in a more considered way, I should, by rights, advise the BGF, the Bloods and Cripps as to the best day to stage your next riot.

You still want to target the end of the month, because EBT cash comes out on the 1st, and also due to the fact that every hoodrat with the last names of Johnson, Jackson and Jefferson are going to get their money on the 14th and 15th. So shoot for the 29th of a 31-day month to kick off your operation, giving all of those J-folk two entire weeks to spend down their free money and get primed to burn the local CVS, to the grounnnn!

Mesc Franklin   September 9, 2015 8:08 PM EDT

Thank you for contributing a dollar to the Freddie Grey foundation!

Joey

Getting Shot in Harm City

DeeJay and I was jus' hangin' out last night, kickin' back, havin' a Mountain Dew, when this dude walked up on us all strapped en shit. He wasn't even lookin' at me or Russell—jus' had eyes on DeeJay.

Russell's like, "Oh shit, dude," and starts to book. Then DeeJay en me roll out and pop, pop, pop! My neck is killin' me, yo. I hope dis shit I got the prescription for take the edge off.

[*Joey is wearing a hospital smock and pajama bottoms and has no shoes as he stands in line at the CVS pharmacy with his script. He is 17, has curly hair and a light tan, and has a bullet wound in the back left side of his neck, where the round grazed his cervical vertebrae, and tore through the muscle, exiting before it hit the artery taking blood to his tiny pea brain. He is stiff, his speech stilted and in pain as he paces from side-to-side, slowly.*]

I don' even know what this shit was about—was jus' hangin' wit da dude when this man stepped to us. Old

The Boned Zone

Dennis came lookin.' He was ready to go off, looking to throw down. But the dude had already rolled—walk up, pop, en go, jus' like that.

'The Suburban Boned Zone'

Man Beaten to Death in Walmart Parking Lot

In the rural and suburban U.S. parking lots are the most dangerous places for a lone person on foot, or in a vehicle. These are asphalt kill boxes. The circumstances surrounding this attack are not clear, so the avoidance tactics available to the victim are uncertain. If this was about a fender bender and these guys were bent on harming him, the only thing he could do is stay in his larger vehicle and either drive to a police station or use it to make hamburger out of these two assholes.

Once he is out of his vehicle, on foot, he's fucked. If you find yourself in this position here are tips on minimizing your damage.

1. Use parked cars to stay away from their vehicle if they are cruising for you. You want them to have to dismount from a distance. The farther they are from their car the shorter their attack window will be.

2. If these guys appear, individually, to be your match, do not stand and fight, but move away obliquely toward cover.

3. Find a shopping cart as soon as possible and use it as a walking barrier.

4. Keep your hands up and out to ward off blows.

5. Do not say anything, ever. If you get hit in the chin while talking you are toast.

6. Realize that there are really dangerous ruthless dudes out there capable of taking you out, who also have friends willing to go along with it. This guy was hit by a pro quality left handed punch to the right eye. This is extremely unusual.

7. If you are hit harder than you have ever been hit and dropped, and or stomped, do not go home. You need to walk into an emergency room and then lay down on the floor between the electric doors so they have to do something with you. The earlier a brain bleed is caught the better your chances of not leaving you woman like this.

Notice the big drive gets out and stops him, then hits him with both hands from a push guard. I'm guessing this dude was a biker, a big dude that knew how to use his size, which is real rare, even among trained fighters. Notice the way that little bastard scrambles out of the passenger side. If a passenger ever exits a vehicle that quick while you are dealing with the driver, run forward past the driver at an angle through obstacles.

These attackers were experienced violent criminals who did not even have time to make a plan, yet carried one out. Study this encounter for parking lot scenarios, not like a karate guy to figure out how to win, but with the mindset of a soldier with only one clip of ammo who does not want to get pinned down in a fire fight. If something like this comes to a fight and you do not have one punch KO power—that's one punch against tough fighters, something most of us lack—and you do not have a knife, then cover your head, move away from the punches and play for time. The farther away from the enemy vehicle you stagger the better.

https://www.youtube.com/watch?v=ytX_0tfSyeI&feature=youtu.be

The Mighty Duck

Black-on-Black Prime Crime

Mondawmin, Baltimore City

Two days ago, at Frederick Douglas High School, home of the Mighty Ducks football team, and of the mob of hoodrats that defeated the Baltimore Police Department in open battle, a thug of 18 years, six feet and two hundred-plus pounds, accused a small [JV corner back I'm guessing] team mate of stealing the visor from his football helmet. This occurred in the school lunch room. The Mighty Duck did not wait for an explanation, but launched a shove-and-punch attack which put the much smaller boy down. He then pinned the small boy's head to a cabinet with his left hand and delivered 13 sloppy, but hard, punches, thrown with his body weight behind them, although he would have been more effective if he kept his elbow in. He then stood, soccer nudged the kid's head with one foot and did a full weight heel stomp with the other foot.

The school police officer responding claimed that the bleeding and unconscious boy was having seizures. The attacker has been charged as an adult with attempted murder and the victim has been released from the hospital. I can tell you that from what I saw of the video that ran as the liberal news casters lied about what was transpiring before our eyes, that if this kid was an amateur boxer he would be barred from sparing or fighting for 180 days. He may have neurological problems for life.

The liberal news caster claimed that the young man had only "allegedly" punched the other, as we watched. He also described the stomp as a step, again, lying to our face to set the proper narrative on its course.

Interestingly enough, had this big thug jock have attacked a white man like this he would have been described as an unarmed teen. Though, having attacked a black teen, he is described as a young man.

It in no way occurred to the press to point out that these very same football players have been given a free pass for hospitalizing 12 police officers back in April. Certainly, this could have nothing to do with the casual nature in which this thug attacked the much smaller boy, and that at least two eye witnesses filmed it instead of interfering with the savage beating.

Welcome to the jungle.

Bernie Hackett   September 23, 2015 9:26 PM EDT

And enfamil, and the Bossa Nova. Oh, and the moon! In the claims field, at certain times of the month, we'd get weird and belligerant calls from the victims. Then the cry would go up-"Is there a full moon?" Definate correlation, folks.

My wife worked as a service rep for BG&E and told similar tales.

We could compare notes as to who had the biggest cloaca maxima for the day.

Unlike me, however, at times Pikesville would lose power, and real drama would ensue! Oy, gevald! Feh! Dry ice! Shriek!

I'd worked the area, myself. It was my education in real drama. I have a well bitten tongue.

Agree, aggravated assault more likely. Maybe he'll get sent to anger management. For him that would be real cruel and unusual punishment. Damn, I'm vicious! Oh, and mean spirited, to boot.

bernie Hackett   September 19, 2015 8:24 PM EDT

JL: When I saw the innocent child's photo on de news, I wondered how large he was. Wonder if he got "held back", 'cause he sure looks old for his grade level.

My overall take on the whole thing was that he was acting naturally. It's probably Bush's fault.

After the news has gone on to better things(?), wonder what he'll get as a punishment?

 **responds:** September 23, 2015 7:41 PM EDT

I actually think the attempted murder charge is overdone. They will have to prove that he planned on killing this kid, and, well, he does not appear to be a person who ever planned a thing in his young dumb life.

Currently, the average size of a 18-year-old black male is six foot and 200 pounds, with that being misleading, as most are either six foot and 150, or six foot and 250.

The average 18-year old white boy is 5' 10" and 230.

Blame it on Similac.

Mandy, Alone

Cast Adrift in Harm City on White Wednesday

Mandy was a deli clerk at an inner city supermarket I managed up until five years ago, which has since fallen into uncaring hands. One will find, in Baltimore, and in this story—related to me by Mandy's mother, as she cried and chain-smoked in her car across the street from my apartment last night—that not caring is a key element in the zombie apocalypse. I'm still sick from the cigarette smoke, but just had to get the story, and she needed to smoke to discuss it.

The first stage is not caring about strangers, an attitude that I have adopted willfully, not even regarding most people as human beings, but slabs of animated meat obstructing my uncaring passage through an unworthy world. Unfortunately, most white men in Baltimore and surrounding municipalities also do not care about their own, particularly their women. For instance, I know one woman who leaves for work from a section of Baltimore City that is overrun with crime at 3 a.m. Both her husband and her adult son, decline to make sure she gets to her car safely. This is the disease of civilization, in which men give over their women and children into the all-protective arms of The State, washing their hands of their primal responsibility to be a protector. When mom walks out the door she's a violent crime statistic that has not happened yet for no reason other than some unarmed black youth has not yet happened upon her as she is leaving the house.

Mandy

It was Mandy's night off. She is a tall, pretty girl with an outgoing personality and long light brown hair. She normally fends for herself going back and forth to work, and on those occasions carried a box cutter. Which, the opinion is, she was lucky not to be carrying. Her mother asked me about this, and I said, "Of the 44 incidents of razor use I have studied, the only time a razor has been decisive is when a person strong enough to deal with the assailant with their empty hands uses it."

Mandy's mother has raised her and her two sisters and brother on her own, because the father is, "a louse," and "a piece of shit." His name is Roger.

Mandy and her unemployed boyfriend, Ethan, wanted to move into together, and since he had no income, they rented a place at Belair Road and Erdman Avenue.

The Boned Zone

Mandy was aware of the reason why virtually every member of her extended family had left Baltimore City. But this was the only place she could afford to rent an apartment, and white guys her age [late teens, early 20s] are rarely employed. So if you want a boyfriend who is not black, you're going to have to support him.

The Belair Edison neighborhood is one of the worst in Baltimore. When I ran into Mandy at the pizzeria, and found out she was living there, I told her to make sure her boyfriend, Ethan, accompanied her when she was out and about.

This past July 8th, a Wednesday Night, at about midnight, on a day when six "bodies were dropped" in our wonderful city, Mandy and Ethan got into an argument. He put her out of the apartment that she rents, in an area where I have been attacked in broad daylight, where I sat on a bus while two Negroes shot another in front of 30 people.

Mandy does carry far too rosy a picture of her fellow humans in her mind's eye. But she was aware of the danger she was in. She had once, when I was still working at the store, been attacked by blacks on an MTA bus, and verbally assaulted by the black bus driver for protesting, and made to walk miles. Her mother's neighbors in the county [two adults with their handicapped son] were attacked last year by eight youths, summoned by a black female bus driver by phone, because they declined to stand with the violent criminals in the back of the bus but remained up front in the handicapped area.

Mandy knew she was in deep trouble, and made a three mile walk to Roger's rental, where he reclines in squalor, supported by his eldest daughter and his Uncle Sam. Roger told his daughter that she should not have been arguing with her boyfriend, that if she hadn't run her mouth, she wouldn't be out on the street.

Mandy's mother was already at work, as she is on the night shift booking arrests at a Central Maryland corrections facility. Mandy, unwelcome at her father's apartment, began walking toward her mother's house, ten miles away in the County. This brought her back through her own neighborhood, about a half mile from where she paid Ethan's rent, through Herring Run Park, where I have had to defend myself with weapons in broad daylight. This is the park I used as the model for Stoner Park in Buzz Bunny, and the Penned in Wild Place in Three-Rivers' Thunder-boy novel. It is not the place for a lone white woman to be, ever, particularly not at night. My Cousin Suzy was once mugged by two black teens here.

The Boned Zone

Getting tired, Mandy sat down at the bus stop at Belair Road and Parkside Drive, thinking she might take a late bus out to Overlea Station and then walk the five miles from there. Overlea Station is bad, and she was keying on that as a safe zone, which shows how skewed people's awareness becomes when they live in an African American Ethical Zone. If you live among criminals, and are not hyper-vigilant—in other words, are not behaving as if you are a war vet suffering from PTSD—then you will begin to adjust your perception in relative terms that will not upset you. This is why most people who are attacked in these areas [most of them being black] are so easy to pick off, because they have sought a happy place in their mind when their environment demands the opposite.

A young black man then attacked Mandy. I will not go into any details. She was grabbed, beaten, clawed, raped at knife point, and told she was going to be killed if she did not stop screaming. Mind you, this is literally happening on a primary street under a municipal traffic light.

After an undetermined length of time, a tall, muscular young man yelled from somewhere on the street and chased off the attacker. He took off his hooded sweat shirt, covered Mandy up with it, asked her where she lived, and then carried her home. The man that carried

Mandy home introduced himself as Marcus, and insisted on not leaving her front door until her boyfriend answered. He then told Ethan what a piece-of-shit he was, and that he had effectively thrown his girl to the dogs, and was as guilty of her attack as if he had done it himself. Ethan would later complain to Mandy that Marcus had hurt his feelings, and that he felt as if he had been unfairly "punked out."

A police officer did respond. He informed Mandy that her boyfriend was someone that she could well do without, and also that she was lucky, because six people had just been killed that day, and she could have easily been number seven.

No arrest has been made based on the sketch of the dude that looks like half the guys in that area.

Marcus literally disappeared. Mandy's mother, a devout catholic, would like to think that Marcus really did disappear, that he was a guardian angel. In my opinion, Marcus, who I have promised to look for so that Mandy's mother can thank him in person, probably had a warrant out on him. He was on foot in the same neighborhood where the other guy was on foot, and that dude, armed with knife, ran like rabbit when Marcus showed up. The subtle implications are that Marcus is what my friend Sandman used to call, "Black niggerbane," which is a subject I'll save for another day.

Mandy's mother called her employer and told her what happened, that Mandy would be out for a week. The employer expressed sympathy and stated that Mandy was their favorite employee, and that the customers "loved her." When Mandy returned to work the black women on staff all came to her and apologized and asked her if there were anything they could do, recommending that she get rid of her boyfriend.

The white women gossiped about her.

One of the black men began following her around making suggestive comments, so she quit, feeling violated by her employer telling her coworkers what had happened, and threatened by the large, black, male coworker stalking her for sex.

Mandy's mother asked me if any of the rentals in my area would be safe for her daughter, and I said, "No! I moved my family out of here and moved back as a bachelor. It's workable for me. We have section eights. This guy here, Binky, is a crack dealer. Down on the end live eleven ex-cons in a halfway house. No white woman should live in Baltimore City unless she has a reliable vehicle and lives with someone who will protect her."

The Boned Zone

Mandy is living with her mother, out in low crime area of Baltimore County, trying to decide how she's going to start over.

In Search of The Boned Zone

Personalizing Your Survival Matrix

Today I told my roommates about recent violence in the neighborhood so that they could adjust their habits accordingly. Then, realizing it was time to review my habitat now that the beat police have been pulled out to beef up courthouse security for the Freddie Gray Memorial Crucifixions, I decided to walk every ambush path in the neighborhood, beginning at 6:03 p.m., and ending at 8:22 p.m.

Someone gets taken down on foot, in Hamilton, every Sunday night. I had no desire to be attacked, but didn't feel right about wrapping up The Boned Zone without at least walking my local ground. I did take my long pointy umbrella with me, so was not unarmed. I chose the umbrella over the 8 inch steel bar because I am primarily concerned about knives.

This would be a meditation on lone nocturnal vigilance, as the lone nocturnal pedestrian is the #1 prey animal in Harm City, the witless creature that is dragged into The Boned Zone with more regularity than any other type or criminal food. The hedges, vine-choked trees, untrimmed shrubs and weed-laced fences made the walk down these many side streets a spooky experience, with the autumn crickets nearly as loud as their summer predecessors.

Foot traffic was light, as was car traffic. Five different police responses could be heard, spaced evenly, with the police chopper doing four extended sweeps of the area.

Everyone on foot was black and alone, except for three pairs and two trios of young black men, and a mother and adult son who were crying about a relative being killed as they staggered down the street arm in arm.

I have just heard another police response—three cars it sounds like, and the chopper is back. I traversed Hamilton, part of Overlea, part of Gardenville, and Part of Cedonia, which scared the shit out of me. I was walking down the middle of the darkened streets overgrown with arching trees and towering weeds, past where Mike the Coke Head caught me in his 71 Super Sport in 1982, and managed to get away without his throat being cut, ten yards down the road from where four boys tried to run me down two months ago, around the corner from where Megan and I almost got swarmed by a pack of hoodrats who veered off at the last moment earlier this year.

Cedonia is terrible. I walked down the alley where Old Man Jimmy fought for his life twice—getting arrested once and KO'd the other time—where a little twerp tried to run me over in a yellow mustang in 1981, where a coworker of mine was beaten to death, where another friend was beaten up by a crack head he arrested, who then climbed the wall and ran along the roof tops of the garages, only to come out on the sidewalk were Jeremy was mugged by two bruthas, cross the street from where Old Man Jimmy's old lady was thrown into the air by a hit and run driver, up the sidewalk past where JR disarmed his black neighbor after he stabbed his white girlfriend in the chest repeatedly on the lawn, across the street from where Big Sam was beaten to death in the church lot alley, past the scene of five pack attacks and armed robberies that is a major hoodrat attack path— seemingly engineered by the City Government to promote violent crime—and finally back up to Hamilton, where the two hoodrats that trailed me two months ago declined to cross Walther, taking me past the house where that 16-year-old black girl was raped to death with a broom stick this past summer, by, you guessed it, a group of black boys—and no one knows her name...

The Boned Zone

White Avenue has hosted a half dozen acts of violence since I moved in five years ago—home, relatively sweet, home.

In a half mile trek I went from a neighborhood where I can point to every single block and name a murder or multiple muggings and beatings, to Hamilton, where crime is steady and nasty but nothing like that.

We had one killing this year.

They had three this year.

It was creepy to walk past vehicles I have used for cover when being pursued on a similarly dark night. However, I was not gathering atmospherics for a horror story, but thinking about the attacks I have documented in this area—and those just as numerous that I have not— while getting a read on the visibility and pacing.

Things are close around here this time of year, a world of weeds and trees waving in the autumn breeze, narrow streets packed with parked cars bumper-to-bumper for blocks.

I'm not being hunted by snipers or archers, or even half-decent hand gunners, but thugs who prefer to beat, stomp and stab as a member of a cohesive pack, so I stay out in the middle of the street.

Even old men with canes are attacked by groups, with rape being about the only one-on-one crime.

Attacks by individuals are—aside from rape—unheard of.

Attacks by pairs are rare.

Attacks by trios are common.

The chopper is doing another search pass.

Attacks by groups of four or more are almost as common as trio attacks.

Shootings, though we have record numbers, are comparatively rare, and mostly involve the drug war.

One in three young black men carry a folding combat knife sold—ironically—on every third corner on the two main streets that bisect Northeast Baltimore. The Pakistani merchants who sell these knives by the case at gas stations and convenience stores price them at $1 an inch, with folders running up to $7. These knives are carried largely because black guys can't fight as well as they used to back in the days before basketball supplanted boxing.

If you are attacked it will be by a group consisting exclusively, or primarily, of young black men, one of whom is more likely than not to be armed with a knife.

My roommate, a karate instructor, suggested dropping one and making the others scatter. There are two problems with this tactic. If the others scatter, the group was not much of a threat in the first place and criminal charges will be placed against you, with the poor oppressed child you decked having two witnesses that saw you jump out of nowhere and attack him.

Fortunately—if you hate lawyers—this is usually not the case. In case after case of attacks by packs of thugs, a pack ethic has been apparent, across the racial board. A surprising level of tenacity has been consistently demonstrated by this enemy, with dozens of men I have interviewed having to fight extended battles, knocking out multiple members of the pack, before the combination of fatigue, casualties and a closing window of opportunity convinced the attackers to retreat.

Silverback was attacked by five to ten young thugs, managed to KO three and hurt another with a shoulder punch, but still had his teeth knocked out by a steel object and had to take a terrible kicking, stomping and punching while striking back with his big hands with his back to his conversion van, kind of like Richard Roundtree as General George Armstrong Custer.

Oliver was attacked by a night club full of fools, who continued to aggress against him for the crime of walking to his car, even after he dropped a fool with a big right hand and threw another one.

When considering white attackers in rural and bar environments in urban enclaves, the individual generally has to KO the entire group—and usually does!

Do not expect your pack attacker to back off after you dropped one dude unless you are armed, and in that case they may then escalate. If one of your attackers heads for a car or building—lookout.

On how exactly lone men successfully slaughter groups of attackers read When You're Food.

For tips on surviving combat read the ongoing serialized books Let the Weak Fall, No B.S. Boxing and Stick Fighting Basics

For now, I live in a city which is stripping deterrence levels of police coverage from residential areas in its quest to appease and put off the mob, even as a mother seeks justice for her nine-year-old son, beaten nearly to death in school, allowed to suffer seizures and slip into a coma in a school chair, only to die in the hospital five days earlier.

No outrage will well up over this crime, which was almost exactly like the death of Freddie Gray, because Black America hates its children, and only pretends to care about their young when Whitey can be taken to task for their fate. The tens of thousands of black boys in Baltimore, being whipped, beaten and punched from cradle to puberty by vicious mothers, without a father to serve as guide or example, understandably hate the world that created them and are willing to strike out at it. While, on many levels, they are pathetic combatants, in an urban environment where the population is disarmed, the packs they form can be as effective as those formed by canines in the wild.

Any attempt to negotiate will fail.

Knocking out one of them will not, in most cases, break the will of the group.

In Harm City or like environs prepare accordingly, with four factors as the pillars of your survival strategy:

1. Functional awareness

2. Behavioral deterrence

3. The ability to incapacitate

4. The tenacity to continue dropping bodies

Good luck.

Death Imitating Fiction

Another Murder in Harm City

In writing the novelette Buzz Bunny, about a bullied boy who finds refuge at an old crime scene at a city park, I used Baltimore's Herring Run Park as the model for the fictional Stoner Park.

Tattoo Rick's Lord of the Fleas story from the 1950s, happened there. [This will be featured on the site this autumn.]

I ducked into that park on three occasions while being pursued by pairs of hood rats, so I could use my nine-inch gravity blade out of sight of witnesses. After the second time I carved a spear from a sapling and cached it there in the Y of a tree by the pumping station.

My cousin Suzy was knocked down and robbed by two black guys there over a decade ago.

This past July 8th a young woman was raped on the street by a knife-armed black man twenty yards from the park.

The Boned Zone

Gun shots ring out every night from Herring Run Park and many other city parks, as they serve as training grounds for the teenage and twenty-something criminals who buy and sell politicians in Baltimore with the fortunes they glean from the War on Drugs.

Yesterday, on the other end of the park, near U.S. Route 40, a cyclist on one of the bike trails found a badly beaten body, so mangled that it could only be identified as male.

A father in the adjoining neighborhood of Armistead Gardens said there have been so many gunshots there at night that he has trained his kids to duck below the windows.

The hipsters moving into Harm City at a 1-4 ratio to those escaping to the suburbs to rent or leaving the state [including five close friends and relatives of mine since April] think that these parks are for their enjoyment, manmade paradises for their gourmet dogs.

But, if we did not have parks, then our corrupt mayor would have to arrange for her sponsors to us police gun ranges and training facilities, and that might be a hard sell even in a city bought and paid for by the drug gangs.*

The City recently expanded outreach programs operated by gang members and affiliates, which serve as grapevines for the criminal underworld, and fewer gang members have been charged with crimes committed during the late April Purge than police officers charged with crimes against gang members in the same time span.

In light of these facts, I think that leaving City parks to the drug gangs was a wise move on the part of the BPD. It's what they are for in this brave new world.

Jeremy Bentham   October 8, 2015 6:58 PM EDT

Life imitating art? Indeed so. In fact our social satires, no matter how outrageous they are intended to be, are steadily becoming uncomfortably close to the truth.

"Federal Government Adds 600,000 Acres To National Forbidden Zone"

http://www.theonion.com/article/federal-government-adds-600000-acres-national-forb-51446

JL **responds:** October 11, 2015 10:18 PM EDT

Dude, I loved Planet of the Apes. Now, thanks to you, I can feel a little more Like Chuck Heston.

'There Was No Fight'

A Case Study in Politically Correct Reporting and Police Work

The following video presentation by the author of 'White Girl Bleed a Lot,' is the only case in which I have seen an actual news reporter, and accredited journalist, fail to abide by the liberal orthodoxy that there is no such thing as an attack, or an assault on a man. The press labels all violence that does not involve guns or feature a female victim of a male aggressor as a "fight."

The pig giving the news conference repeatedly uses the term fight, which has no place in a law enforcement statement, as what sane people regard as a fight is legally a "mutual combat," and manifestly not the beating of a small youth by a mob of adults and youths.

I have not seen clearer evidence than this video that municipal law enforcement personnel are in league with the vile media.

https://www.youtube.com/watch?v=-cbO8wuF6VQ

PR   November 22, 2015 6:59 PM EST

I don't think the cop actually believes there was a 'fight' as opposed to a beating. He wants certain people to come forward or the community to give them up. If he tells the community, "We want these people to assess their culpability in an assault," the people are a lot less likely to turn them in. If he says what he did, "we want to talk to them," he might get a response. He also has to deal with a hostile yuppie white press, so his statements have to be tailored for them. He's in the business of persuasion and evidence gathering.

I'd imagine he has to go home and take a shower after saying these things but he does what he must. Not all cops in all jurisdictions are like Baltimore PD.

 **responds:** November 30, 2015 4:42 PM EST

I agree with your take on this cop. He seemed to regret half of what came out of his mouth, like some feminist bitch ad her hand up his ass controlling his speech through tweaks of his spinal chord.

I saw another media/police claim that an assault was a fight in the paper, and then on the news at thanksgiving. It seems to be conquest by semantics.

Mapping The Boned Zone

Notes on Using A Mobile Map Index

My son showed me on his smart phone this crime icon system that places symbols on a map of your locale to give you a heads up on what kind of crime is happening in the area. Charles and I are currently working on a supplement—actually a base line template for the use of—such indexes.

Here is why:

According to the violence survey I did between 1996 and 2000, 29% of violence found its way into a police report or civil suit. Let's make that 25% probably made its way into the FBI database.

From 2010-2015 only 10% of the violence I have documented has resulted in "legalities," therefore whatever index you are using, since it is based on law enforcement stats, is just the tip of the aggression iceberg. The great myth of our generation was that violent crime was reducing even as it expanded, a myth perpetrated by our media and law enforcement.

To use such indexes, which are subject to police statistical manipulation due to political pressure, I suggest the following:

Know who the people who report the crimes are.

The people who report arrests are the cops. Most arrests are for drug possession or sale. For every such arrest there will be numerous violent crimes that go unpunished and unreported, committed by both the users and sellers of these substances. So, when you see a cluster of arrest markers, you must consider that area a war zone of sorts, with 10 to 40 times the violence indicated by the arrest icon.

Burglaries are actually an indication that teenage criminals addicted to drugs are living in an upscale community, which is no surprise. This data is only pertinent if you plan on buying a home there.

Robbery and assaults are often misreported, but can generally be lumped into people using aggression against other individuals. Attacks by groups on individuals rarely make it into crime stats, but occur roughly 10 times as often as reported robberies in an area.

The Boned Zone

The people reporting robberies and assaults are generally middle class folks who believe—falsely—that the police will do something to help. Poor and working class people hardly bother to report crimes because they now the police are not inclined or able to help. Also, many working class crime victims—like a friend of mine who was fingerprinted for reporting the burglary of his apartment—are harassed by cops, and accused of committing some crime that they are trying to cover up by filing a police report.

Therefore, if you are a middle class person of the type who might consider reporting a crime on your person, than icons indicating robbery and assault are a sign that people like you are being targeted by violent criminals at roughly the frequency indicated by the map.

Shootings are generally reported at the highest level, with one of every three shootings reported in Baltimore, Maryland for instance. In an urban area multiply shootings by three to get the probably rate of actual lead dispersal.

The only crime that is reported at or near the actual rate of occurrence is homicide.

The Boned Zone

Check out this smart phone app below, and if you know of any others please post a link in the comment section below.

http://m.spotcrime.com/mobile/map/index.html#

Ron Bone in the Hood

Finding The Boned Zone: Part 1

When I was 18, and had just moved to Baltimore, a big sasquatch looking dude nick-named Ron Bone, who worked in the grocery store where I had just landed a job, offered to rent me a room—a couch, actually—for half my pay, about $50 per week. Thus I ended up living in a stoner apartment over top of the Golden Key diner and the Wilken's House bar. As a non drug user with a big knife, I was the watchdog, living at the end of the long hallway above the unlooked door to the narrow stair where Ron Bone's drug dealers, biker buddies, and sluts, would call at any time. The other two dudes were Paul—legally insane and on SSI—and Dave, a man whore whose girlfriend paid his portion of the rent. They each had a room.

Ron Bone had an XT-500 dirt/street bike that we used for our transportation. He looked like a gorilla on a tricycle on this thing. I sat my narrow ass on the back and carried our beer, and our groceries, and our beer, and occasionally Christmas presents for our mothers and friends, earning undying fame for falling off the back of the bike at a stop light, but saving the beer as my back smacked on the asphalt and my body cushioned the fall of the bottled nectar of our suicidal gods. This six months of living with the giant degenerate pseudo-biker was quite an experience. All of his friends and our co-workers were stoners. I was the only one that only drank—and that was new for me. When people would try to talk me into getting high, Ron Bone would say, "No, don't—he's already there. This is the only dude I can talk to when I'm tripping."

Well, Ron Bone would drink a case of beer, eat a bunch of acid, smoke a bong, maybe take a horse tranquilizer, and then "Go out on a mission."

He liked the fact that I did not get involved in his insane crime sprees, which kind of made me a priest-chronicler at his stoned midnight confession. He came back in the middle of the night with books [he robbed a catholic book store to get me some religious books, which I returned], CB radios, stereos, TVs, potted plants and even angels, Virgin Mary's and gargoyles from graveyards and churches. He would then hide this stuff and tell me his story, so I could tell it back to him the next day while he began to get drunk again. The missions were like his amnesiac dream quests.

The Boned Zone

Ron Bone could drink a case of wine or two cases of beer without pissing. He would then wake up and piss for so long that the toilet would flush from the added volume. His was not a healthy lifestyle. I was the beer guy, only paying half rent, hauling the beer, and chopping firewood on the living room floor where I slept—usually in the from of railroad ties that we dragged up out of the parking lot around back. The flew in the chimney did not work, so you would have to sit on the floor or die. This was cold winter 80/81, I think.

The long access hallway from the stairs was only 2.5 feet wide. Ron Bone, in a rare show of industry, applied Stucco to this long narrow hallway. I didn't get it, until, the morning after one of his five weekly parties. That morning, as I hid my bowie knife in a couch cushion so it wouldn't be stolen while I was at work, he said, "Hey Mork [his nickname for me], let's check and see how good the party was last night."

We found flannel at shoulder level, some skin, denim at hip level, and even a tuft of blond hair, the sight of which pleased him greatly.

Ron Bone was evil.

One night he drank me under the table—not that we actually had one—and went out for "a mission!" I had a first aid kit, so when he came home slashed up he tried to revive me to treat him and failed, wrapping the gashed open forearm in one of Bone Head's [his side kick with the car he used to transport stolen goods and dope, who did not even possess a real name] jackets and passed out next to me.

The next day, as we duct taped his forearm closed, he told me what had happened.

He rode out and tried to steel a lawn mower, but felt conspicuous hauling it on his bike. He dropped it when two guys in a pickup tried to run him over for stealing it, and sped off into the city. He rode, and rode and rode, until he ended up in this run down neighborhood with no cars, with seemingly nothing worth stealing. He pulled up to this crowd of dudes drinking whiskey and smoking dope in the middle of a street and asked them for directions.

They ignored him.

He said, "What are you stupid?"

Three of the guys turned to look at him, a white guy, and two black guys. In response to their stares he said, "Of course your stupid—you're partying with niggers."

Then, all dozen or so of the men turned and looked at him, all black except the first man, and he said, apologetically, "Oh, you *are* niggers."

They rushed him, and by the time he got his bike wheeled around and throttled it one was running beside him and slashed open his left forearm with a razor or knife. The gash seemed kind of wide for a razor to me.

We went to work, and then went drinking that night at a place that had a giant stuffed polar bear in the lobby. After eating two horse tranquilizers Ron Bone danced with the bear. Eventually, in some frightening dive, we met up with some Lumbee Indian bikers in Highlandtown. They didn't like the looks of me. But after he assured them that I was the most insane person he knew, they decided I could live. I had no idea how manipulative this guy was, or yet understood that he was a physical coward, cunning diplomat and convincing story teller, who was cultivating an image for me as his psychotic—stab you in the alley—twerp assassin.

Although he was a hulking athletic man, he never, ever used his size to intimidate and always practiced soft "I'm your best friend" diplomacy. I think he was 22, having just dropped out of College.

I was under his counter-culture spell, which did not seem so bad since we both hated the world and he—degenerate though he was—did not try to get me to compromise my ethics, or so I thought, and pointed to my "weird 'Mork from Ork' honor code" as the key to our friendship. I was, of course, being played, but still had a year before I figured it out.

Bernie Hackett   October 9, 2015 6:50 PM EDT

JL:

The stuffed polar bear was in the entrance to Sourises, in Towson. I remember it from my drinkin' daze.

I haven't thought of that in years.

I remember thinking that was fairly unusual, particularly for Towson, which wasn't trendy in them days.

Strange days!

responds: October 11, 2015 10:44 PM EDT

I knew it began with an S—thanks!

Rone Bone and the Man

Finding the Boned Zone: Part Two, Conclusion

After spending a winter without heat in the dive apartment, Ron Bone and I moved into Bone Head's house that spring, and the corner of Bayonne and Bella Vista became a scene of a party every night but Thursday. The parties were "bring your own bottle." As the host, Ron Bone drank some of this and some of that.

His gorgeous girlfriend, who was Italian and Indian, [I've known one other Indian Italian mix and she's beautiful too, even at 70] and a figure skating instructor, would come over on Thursday night while we drank the left over beer and I cleaned my AR-7 and 20-guage and sharpened and oiled my bowie knife and meat hook. We went out shooting at what he insisted was a legal range, every Thursday afternoon. It turned out to be some drug dealer's property, which I found out when Bone Head and I ventured there on our own one day and ended up looking down the barrel of an assault rifle.

Ron's girl was only allowed to wear a shirt. No panties, leg covering or footwear were allowed. He used to beat her savagely when I wasn't around, and she would keep coming back. He had a cat who smoked pot and drank, which he named Charlie Manson and he had trained to attack her legs. When he sent her downstairs for a beer the cat would wait and she would sneak until the cat pounced and then she was off and running for the beer, and back up the stairs. Ron Bone explained that she was "funny about her legs" since she was a figure skater, and that this method of his served the greater good because it entertained Charlie and made sure his beer was cold.

One night I came home to an empty house and heard Ron Bone's plaintive voice from his bedroom. I entered and saw him sprawled across his water bed. He sat up with a huge knot on his forehead. Apparently, his girl had refused to go for another beer after Charlie got her once, and when he began to rise from the bed to make good on his threat to throw her down the stairs [one time he threw her down the stairs and as she stood out on the lawn and cussed him, threw stolen graveyard statuary at her from his bedroom window] she picked up his favorite reefer ash tray, a star-shaped glass thing that weighed "pounds" and hit him in the forehead with it, and left him out cold.

He admired her for the spunk and thought what she had done to him was commendable and hilarious. She would be back. Rone Bone had something that few males beyond the equine order possessed in such abundance, and she never seemed to break that spell.

Well, with his girl out of the picture that week, he broke his promise to me and invited dozens of people over that I did not know. I took my guns and knives up to my tiny bedroom which had no door and was next to the bathroom, and cleaned and sharpened my entire collection. Eventually, unable to get to sleep, I went downstairs and confronted Ron Bone about the crowd and the noise. He seemed contrite, even backed away from me in fear, and asked me to please not be mad.

I returned upstairs, then after about five minutes, I felt kind of bad about ruining his night, and beside, had noticed a girl that I fancied who had been looking at me while I confronted him, and decided to go join the party and commit to waking up to a hangover at six in the morning while Ron Bone filled the toilet to the flush mark with a night's unreleased urine.

I went downstairs, putting my shirt on first, so as not to seem like such a nutty hillbilly, and stepped into an empty living room with half drunk beer bottles all about. Ron Bone was standing in the kitchen with the refrigerator door open—the door to our ever-empty beer cooler—with a big grin on his face, humming his favorite Yes song to himself and stamping his feet as he made his selection.

I asked him where everybody went.

He said, "Well, Mork, after you went upstairs someone asked me who you were and why you were so pissed. I said, 'Oh, that's my roommate, the one that lives at the top of the stairs and cleans his guns and knives all day. He was pissed about the party.' It took them thirty seconds to clear the house—they left enough beer for the week!"

It was a set up from the beginning, so I grew wary of Ron Bone including me in anything. I was becoming the psychotic maniac who lived with the cool party host.

The Man

One day, Ron Bone, having borrowed his girl's car, offered to drive me around and run whatever errands I needed done, so we did so, getting myself a new pair of work boots. Then, as we sat at a traffic light, he said, "Hey, Mork, John is meeting me at this guy's office. I lost track of time—need to be there in ten minutes. Could you come?"

"Dude, is this a drug deal?"

The Boned Zone

"No, I wouldn't do that to you, Mork—promise."

We pulled up at the first office building in Towson off of Joppa Road, just past the Black and Decker building. John, a biker, was there, with a Hobart meat scale in the bed of his pickup truck. Ron Bone picked it up like it was nothing and asked me to hold the door for him, as we walked toward the door that didn't need held because some dude in a suit was holding it and John was grousing in the background about some "crazy shit."

The suit walked us to an elevator in this posh building and let us in. When Ron Bone and I were in the elevator he said, "Are you packing one of your knives?"

"No, I was going shopping for shoes!"

"Do you have any kind of weapon?"

I palmed an ink pen, the first time I can recall imagining a writing implement as a weapon since stabbing this big dude in front of Mister Richardson on my first day of high school.

He frowned, "Can you stop someone with that?"

"Unlikely, if he's as fit and alert as the guy in the lobby."

The Boned Zone

I was pissed and he was literally sweating, worry written on his face.

Another suit ushered us into what was not an office, but a penthouse apartment, where a wimpy looking thirty-year-old dude with soft brown hair and watery blue eyes, who was dressed like some rich brat on vacation, sat on a couch. He motioned for Ron Bone to place the scale on the coffee table in front of him, as the second suited guy, a dude with a blonde crew cut and a thick neck, who I figured would make short work of me, stood with his back to the door looking directly at me as I paced back and forth, his hands folded before his belt buckle.

Ron Bone and this watery-eyed rich guy had a low muffled negotiation which I did not want to hear, and tuned out, while I glared at the muscle guy in the suit who was blocking the way out while I paced back and forth. Eventually I heard friendly words, saw a hand shake out of the corner of my eye, and felt relief as Ron Bone's giant hand came down on my shoulder and the man before us stepped aside to let us leave.

When we got into the hallway Ron Bone ran for the stairs and I followed, running down behind him, hustling out through the lobby, and getting into his girl's car and pulling off as quickly as possible. I never knew he was that damned quick. As we pulled off I was relieved but angry, and just glared at him. He apologized, pulled over, showed me 17 hundred dollar bills, and gave me one. I took it and resolved to use it as part of a security deposit for my own place, making a mental note never to go anywhere with Ron Bone again.

The Den

I soon stopped drinking, moved out, got a place with my wife to be, and then realized, I had left my shotgun behind at Bone Head's place, and that, it being a perfect home defense weapon, I should retrieve it.

I had a wool army surplus blanket to wrap it up in, and walked the two miles to his place. When I knocked on the door some big, tattooed, bearded, biker I did not recognize answered the door. I just said, "I came for my shotgun."

He nodded and let me in. There were about five bikers lounging around smoking and drinking with five mostly naked chicks who looked like they should have been in high school, not with a bunch of bikers ten years older than me.

The Boned Zone

They were watching the Mel Gibson movie The Road Warrior.

I picked my way through the alternately dainty and leather-clad bodies, saw the 20 gauge still on the rack in the dining room over Bone Head's 1898 8 mm Mauser, wrapped it up as the lead guy watched, nodded to him, and walked out past him, assuming Ron Bone was bedded down with someone upstairs.

That was not my last dealing with Ron Bone, but after standing next to him in that elevator as he sweated and contemplated selling some stolen merchandise to someone he was afraid of, I was done with Ron Bone as a friend.

The Boned Zone

Sir, the walkway ends there—Please, step away from The Boned Zone!